BEGINNINGS

A Collection of Appetizers Presented by

the Junior League of Akron

The City of Akron, Ohio

Since its inception, Akron, Ohio, has been a community of beginnings—many of which are highlighted throughout this book. In that same spirit, so too has the Junior League of Akron been an organization of beginnings, developing and donating numerous charitable projects to benefit the hometown we love so well. What better way to express our enthusiasm and continued support than by offering this special collection of appetizers, the beginnings of so many meals and gatherings, to all of you. Profits from the purchase of this cookbook will benefit the continued charitable efforts of the Junior League of Akron and its projects.

© Rick Zaidan, University of Akron's Goodyear Polymer Center

© Rick Zaidan, courtesy of Stan Hywet Hall and Gardens

© Rick Zaidan, Canal Park Stadium

Published by the Junior League of Akron, Ohio, Inc.

Copyright © 2000 by the Junior League of Akron, Ohio, Inc.
All rights reserved.

This book, or any portions thereof, may not be reproduced in any form without written permission of the Junior League of Akron. Any inquiries should be directed to the Junior League of Akron, 929 West Market Street, Akron, Ohio 44313.

(330) 836-4905

Printed in the United States of America
Favorite Recipes® Press
an imprint of

FRP
1-800-358-0560

First Printing: 2000 12,500 copies

ISBN: 0-9671721-0-1
Library of Congress Catalogue Number: 99-095373

13 *Casual*

Perfect for relaxed entertaining, the culinary creations found in this collection—delectable dips, savory spreads and other extraordinary casual fare—are sure to be crowd-pleasers for your family and friends.

BEGINNINGS

79 *Classic*

Well-known recipes, and those soon to be famous, are featured in this compilation of our favorite tried-and-true, traditional appetizers, which are easy to make and even easier to devour. Always in fashion, most recipes transition smoothly from casual get-togethers to more elegant soirées.

113 *Elegant*

When only the best will do, the appetizers and hors d'oeuvres featured in this special section are exceptional for more refined gatherings—the "to-die-for" first course at a candlelit dinner, magnificent morsels for grazing at a cocktail party, savory tidbits passed on silver trays, and much more. Luxurious, tasteful entertaining never tasted this good.

Pictured on the cover

(right to left, front cover to back cover)

Scotch Salmon Canapés (recipe on page 122)

Pesto and Orzo-Stuffed Cherry Tomatoes (page 50)

Snow Peas with Boursin (page 140)

Summit Sunburst (page 89)

Fruit Kabob with Raspberry Cream Fruit Dip and

Ginger and Lime Fruit Dip (pages 39 and 34)

Credits and Acknowledgments

Beginnings *was completed because of the dedication and shared vision of many individuals. Our deepest gratitude goes to all of those listed here and to anyone that we may have inadvertently failed to mention. The Junior League of Akron is grateful to the following, who joined with us to promote the success of* Beginnings *and to further our good works in the community.*

Cookbook design: The Cookbook Design
　　Committee, Babcock, Schmid,
　　Louis & Partners Design
Food and Akron photography: Rick Zaidan
Food Styling: Barbara S. Churchill and
　　Suzanne Bonhomme Locke
Junior League of Akron President 1998–99:
　　Brenda Burnham Unruh
Junior League of Akron President 1999–2000:
　　Patricia Blackstone
Members of the Board of Directors
History and sidebar material:
　　Akron-Summit County Library
　　Michael Cohill
　　Tom Hollingsworth of Inventure Place
　　John A. Kuhar
　　John Z. Miller, University of Akron
　　　　Archives
　　Charles E. Renner, Sr.
　　Summit County Historical Society
　　Mark Williamson, director of
　　　　communications for Mayor Donald J.
　　　　Plusquellic, City of Akron
　　Patricia Milestone Zonsius

Steering Committee
Chairman and Editor:
　　Patti Kuhar Renner
Assistant Chairman: Jaclyn Freeman Donenwirth
Recipe Co-Chairman: Laura Botto Comstock
Recipe Co-Chairman: Amy Hadley Glessner
Marketing Chairman: Suzanne Bonhomme Locke
Assistant Marketing Chairman:
　　Cheryl Streicher Rauch
Design Chairman: Barbara S. Churchill
Controller: Kathy Vereecken Lane
Special Assistance: Courtney Farr

Committee Members
Beth Allen
Barbara Crouse Babbitt
Heather Benson
Loren Lytle Brunemann
Tina Nichols Buehrle
Colleen Cochrun
Katarina Vujic Cook
Roberta Kleinman DeBarr
Kristine Fonte
Carrie Hoover
Kirsten Robinson King
Amy Comunale Klein
Michelle DiCresce Luecke
Suzanne Manby
Susan M. Mann
Margaret Mehigan
Nikki Moshier
Sarah Castle Rossi
Anne-Marie Sawicki
Monica Comunale Stevens
Lorrie Thompson-Bossart
Marguerite Dannemiller Tremelin

Our Beginnings

For the past 75 years, the Junior League of Akron has worked diligently to meet the needs of the community as is reflected by its mission statement:

The Junior League of Akron empowers women for positive change in our community.

The Junior League of Akron began in 1923 as the Junior Charity League, founded with 67 members who wanted to make a difference in the community. The core of the Charity League was formerly the Babies Aid Society of Children's Hospital. In 1926, the Junior Charity League was accepted into The Association of Junior Leagues International, Inc. and became the Junior League of Akron, Ohio. Today, this strong organization of trained volunteers boasts over 600 members committed to the shared vision of being "recognized as a leading catalyst and partner in creating collaborative solutions for community change."

Over the years this vision has fueled many beginnings from which the community has benefited. As from the start, Junior League of Akron members continue to donate their time, talent, and energy to a number of community projects to help make our area a better place. The list on the following page reflects a few of the many projects that were started, refined, and transferred to the community for ongoing operation thanks to the financial and volunteer resources from the Junior League of Akron.

1920s

Akron City Hospital Book Collection/Carts
Children's Hospital Book Collection/Carts
Bowen/Goodrich Schools Occupational
    Therapy Program
Mary Day Nursery

1930s

Katherine McLain Knight Nursery
East Akron Community House
Aid to Dependent Children
Akron Health Department
Well Baby Clinic
Akron Child Guidance Center

1940s

World War II Volunteer Efforts: Red Cross/Motor
    Corps, USO, nurses aides and Grey Ladies
Volunteer Service Bureau (The Volunteer Center)

1950s

Child Welfare Survey
"Patches and Quilts" Publication
Homemaker Service
Akron Recreation Department Show Wagon
Children's Gallery at the Akron Art Institute

1960s

Mental Health Educational Seminars and Rallies
The Henry and Grace School Learning
    Resource Center
Family Living Institute
Planned Parenthood Association
"Direction" Booklet for the Handicapped
Health Museum
Pre-School Therapy Unit at Akron Child
    Guidance Center

1970s

Motor Perceptual Project
Health Education Center
Summit County Toy and Resource Center
International Film and Television
    Festival of New York
        Award Winning "City at the Summit"
Going Places
Safe Landing Runaway Shelter
Child Abuse Awareness Project
Akron Art Substitute (Artmobile)

1980s

Mentorship Program Coalition
Realistic Parenting ("What's Next?
    You and Your Baby")
Guardian Ad Litem
Institute for Child Advocacy
Guardian Improvement Program
Scholarship Fund
Family Recovery Center
Junior Leadership Akron
Safe Landing Youth Shelter for Girls
Sexuality: Parent and Kids Talk
Battered Women's Shelter

1990s

The Volunteer Fair
The Oral Health Initiative
The Immunization Coalition of Summit County
Kaleidoscope
Family T.I.E.S. (partnering with Akron
    Child Guidance Center)

Tasters and Testers

Each recipe in this collection has been prepared and evaluated by so many individuals and their families and friends. Our thanks to all of those listed here and to anyone that we may have inadvertently failed to mention.

Kara Alvey
Lori Ashton
Barbara Crouse Babbitt
Craig M. Babbitt
Gina Bisesi
Patricia C. Blackstone
William M. Blackstone
Beau and Don Botto
Cobe Botto
Vicki and David Brockman
Tina Buehrle
Candace Campbell
Marlene and Paul
     Campbell
Janet Caplinger
Judy Cendro
Anne Churchill
Barb Churchill
Suzanne P. Clayton
Colleen Cochrun
Melissa Cohill
Laura B. Comstock
Richard W. Comstock
W. Cooper Comstock
Megan Conrad
Katarina and Kevin Cook
Laura and Robert Culp
Kelly Cunningham
Paula Cutillo

Lisa Dannemiller
Brenda L. Davison
Roberta Kleinman DeBarr
Alexa Deininger
Ian Donenwirth
Jackie Donenwirth
Karl Donenwirth
Mira Donenwirth
Alice and John Edminister
Debby Eisinger
Stephanie Ferrara
Jack Gillman
Alex Glessner
Amy Glessner
Dan Glessner
Hayley Glessner
Jerry Godic
Amy Goodwill
Craig Griffin
Alan Hadley
Louise Hadley
Maryrosa and Scott Hamed
Amy and Tom Hissong
Carrie Hoover
Mary and Wellborn Jack
Michelle Kaser
Bob Kerr
Kirsten and Andrew King
Lou Ellen Kirkendall

Nancy Koly
Laurie Krutz
Kathy Lane
Bob Lang
Pat Lang
Adam LeMonier
Heather and Ross Licata
Sue and Kevin Locke
Michelle and Fred Luecke
Laurie Luketic
Norma Lute
Lisa and Doug MacKay
Suzanne Manby
Bill Mann
Joan Mann
Susan Mann
Sheila and Dan McBride
Peggy McCoy
Bobbie Camp McGloin
Elizabeth McGrath
James McKenzie
Sue and John McKenzie
Sue R. McKenzie
Melinda McMillan
Margaret Mehigan
Denise and Tim
     Merryweather
Karen Migchelbrink
Cheryl K. Murphy

Sue Danna Myer
Chris Nonno
Lou Nonno
Laurie Oravecz
Melissa Ost
Carmen Oyenque
Caitlin Papajcik
Dale Papajcik
Jill Papajcik
Chris Petracca
Sally Phillips
Kimberly A. Platt
Debbie Prinz
Karen Quilon
Judy Ramsier
Cheryl and Greg Rauch
Maggie and Pete Reagan
Audrey and John Renner
Patti and Bob Renner
Samuel Shotwell Renner
Jan Rice
Patrice Leeds Richman
Ann and Jeff Robson
Alita Rogers
Cathy Rumble
Patty Saks
Diane and George Sarkis
Donna Schobert
Jeff Schobert
Jerry Schobert
Jessica Schobert
Kathy Schobert
Peg Schobert

Recipe Contributors

Ryan Schobert
Steve Schobert
Kathy Scott
Carol Seiler
Gloria Seiler
Robert Seiler
Kathy Shisler
Mary Jane Stanchina
Monica Comunale
　　Stevens
Ed Stockton
LuAnne Stockton
Gary Thompson
Jane Thompson
Melinda Topliff
Val and Jon Torrens
Amy and Eric Treend
Marguerite Tremelin
Brenda Burnham Unruh
Debbie Urban
Mike Urban
Debbie Walsh
Andre Walters
Tanya Walters
Barbara and Jeff Warner
Shelly A. Webb
Alice and Charles Wilkes
Julie and Mark Wilkes
Kim and Matt Wilkes
Melissa Wilkes
Lara Stockwell Wilson
Terri Zavoda
Pat Zeigler

We thank the many women of the Junior League of Akron for sharing their favorite appetizer recipes with us. We regret that we did not have room for them all in the book.

Nancy Aleman
Constance L. Anderson
　　(Mrs. Frank)
Jean M. Anderson
Lori Ashton
Mary Bauer
Christine Beckner
Judy Cendro
Bonnie Childs
Barbara S. Churchill
Laura B. Comstock
Katarina Vujic Cook
Paula R. Cutillo
Polly Davis
Brenda L. Davison
Roberta Kleinman DeBarr
Catherine K. Durkin
Betty Eastman
Elena Economou
Johnna Economou
Debby Eisinger
Ruth Forsyth
Ruthie Friedman
Katie George
Amy Glessner
Rita Howard
Mary Fearon Jack
Nawzat Kakish-Fisher
Nancy A. Koly

Joan M. Kramer
Judy Kukk
Marylee Lewis
Cathie Lippincott
Margaret Lloyd
Tracey Lloyd
Sue Locke
Michelle Luecke
Lisa MacKay
Suzanne Manby
Carolyn Marting
Sheila McBride
Bobbie Camp McGloin
Sue R. McKenzie
　　(Mrs. James W.)
Gia Meadows
Margaret Mehigan
Lisa Millisor
Cheryl Murphy
Laurie Oravecz
Melissa Ost
Jan Parry
　　(Mrs. George T.)
Rebecca Pool
Cheryl Rauch
Kathleen George Renner
Patti Kuhar Renner
Ann Robson
Cathy Rumble

Pam Ryan
Carol Sankovic
Anne-Marie Sawicki
Laura Stockslager
Jane Thompson
Amy Treend
Brenda Burnham Unruh
Carolyn VonWyl
Kris Wagner
Shelly Webb
Melissa Wilkes
Rebecca Zurava

Foods in Bloom

A Listing of Edible Flowers

Allium

A perennial herb that blooms during May and June with pretty lilac-pink flowers that can be used, in addition to the hollow leaves, as a garnish or substitute for scallions.

Bee Balm

Bees and hummingbirds are attracted to this citrus-tasting herb whose leaves and colorful scarlet flowers can be used with fruits, duck, and pork, or in salads, teas, and jellies.

Borage

The bright blue star-shaped flowers have a cucumber-like flavor and are often used in salads. The flowers may also be floated in drinks or candied for a dessert garnish.

Calendula

The ray petal is the edible portion of the blossom and provides an attractive garnish. It is often used to color butter and cheese and is commonly known as the pot marigold. It can be used as a substitute for saffron and has a tangy, peppery taste.

Clove Pinks

This wild ancestor of the modern carnation has a spicy, mild clove flavor. The semi-double fragrant flowers of this perennial can be used fresh to flavor syrups, fruit cups, or beverages, but be sure to remove the bitter white base first.

Daisy

A perennial flower that has a mild flavor, the daisy can be eaten fresh in salads or used as a garnish.

Dandelion

This familiar yellow flower can be minced and added to butters, spreads, and vinegar.

Day Lily

The yellow, tawny orange flowers of all day lilies are edible, but sample first to determine taste before chopping into salads or soups. Pick the flower buds after they have elongated but before they open, as the smaller buds tend to taste better.

Fennel

Fennel's mild licorice-flavored leaves and large yellow ublema flowers should be used fresh, not dried, in soups and salads.

Scented Geraniums

A perennial grown as an annual or houseplant, these come in a wide variety of colors and scents, which are released by being rubbed or by the hot sun. Use for baked goods, ice creams, jellies, candied garnishes, and scented sugar.

Hollyhocks

The flowers are best used as an attractive container for a dish or as a garnish, but can also be made into fritters or flavoring for tea.

Honeysuckle

Known for its delightful fragrance and sweet taste, the honeysuckle can be used in puddings, ice creams, or syrups.

Johnny-jump-ups

These flowers make a pretty candied garnish on a dessert or can brighten up a spring salad or punch bowl. Their mild taste is reminiscent of sweet baby lettuce.

Lavender

A perennial shrub with graceful purple flowers and a scent that is associated more with potpourri than cooking. However, its leaves and flowers can be used in vinegar or jellies, or used sparingly in salads, ice creams, and custards.

Lilac

The pyramidal lavender clusters of its flowers are known for their scent, which carries over into their taste, and can be candied or used in herb butters, scented sugars, or as a garnish. The blossoms should be picked as soon as they open.

Marigold

Although all are edible, the Tangerine Gem and Lemon Gem varieties have a more pleasant flavor; there is a Peruvian variety used in salsa. Most marigolds are a good accompaniment to salads, soups, and sauces.

Nasturtium

The slightly peppery taste of the young leaves, flowers, and buds, combined with their vibrant colors, brighten any green salad. The flowers also provide a unique container for cold salads, but the bitter-tasting base should be removed first.

Pansy

Similar in taste to Johnny-jump-ups, the flowers are often used as a garnish on desserts or floating in cold drinks or soups. They should be picked when they first open.

Pineapple Sage

Rough, dark green leaves and bright scarlet tubular flowers that bloom in late summer characterize this tender perennial. The flowery, pineapple taste, with a hint of sage muskiness, can season fruit salads, tea, desserts, and tea breads.

Roses

Older varieties seem to have more scent and therefore more taste, but many varieties can be quite bitter, so sample first. The hips and petals can be used for making tea, jelly, jam, syrup, or wine. The petals can also be candied or used to make rosewater, scented sugar, or butter.

Squash Blossoms

The golden-orange flowers should be picked when fully open, but don't pick them all, or there'll be no squash! The blossoms can be chopped into soups, salads, or vegetable dishes. Be sure to remove stamens and pistils before cooking.

Sweet Woodruff

A staple of the May punch bowl, the tiny star-shaped white flowers of this shade-loving perennial can also garnish tea cakes, desserts, salads, and fruits, especially berries.

Thyme

The lilac-colored flowers tend to be mild with a floral scent, perfect for garnishing salads, pastas, or desserts.

Tulip

Like the nasturtium, these brightly colored flowers are best used as a garnish or container for a cold dish, such as chicken or egg salad. Their light flavor is similar to peas. The best variety for culinary use is the Darwin hybrid.

Violet

Like the Johnny-jump-up and pansy, this hardy perennial has a sweeter, stronger scent. Its flowers and heart-shaped leaves can be used as a garnish. The flowers can be made into violet water, which can flavor tea, breads, fruit compotes, and chilled soups.

Wine and Cheese Complements

	Wine	Cheese		Wine	Cheese
White	Chablis Chardonnay Chenin Blanc Moselle Pouilly Fuisse Riesling Sauterne Sauvignon Blanc Soave	Boursin Brie Camembert Creamy Bleu Gouda Gruyère Montrachet Port Salut Roquefort	**Appetizer**	Blush Champagne Sherry Vermouth	Cheddar Fontina Gorgonzola Gruyère Port Salut
Red	Beaujolais Bordeaux Burgundy Cabernet Sauvignon Chianti Claret Rosé Zinfandel	Bel Paese Cheddar Edam Monterey Jack Piquant Bleu Roquefort Swiss Tilsit	**Sparkling**	Champagne Cold Duck Sparkling Burgundy Sparkling Rosé	Any of the cheeses listed at left, under Appetizer, Red, or White Wine, would also be appropriate complements to any of the sparkling wines.
			Dessert	Cream Sherry Muscatel Port Sweet Sherry Tokay	Brie Camembert Cheddar Cream Liederkranz Roquefort Stilton

"Small cheer and great welcome
makes a merry feast."

—*William Shakespeare*

appetizers

casual

In This Section

Chocolate Coffee Punch

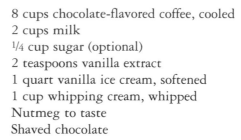

8 cups chocolate-flavored coffee, cooled
2 cups milk
1/4 cup sugar (optional)
2 teaspoons vanilla extract
1 quart vanilla ice cream, softened
1 cup whipping cream, whipped
Nutmeg to taste
Shaved chocolate

Combine the coffee, milk, sugar and vanilla in a bowl, stirring until the sugar dissolves. Place the ice cream in a punch bowl. Pour the coffee mixture over the ice cream. Top with the whipped cream. Sprinkle with nutmeg and chocolate shavings. Ladle into punch cups. Yield: 16 servings.

The invention of the ice cream cone is attributed to Charles E. Menches of Akron in 1903. According to legend, the young ice cream salesman at the Louisiana Purchase Exposition gave an ice cream sandwich and flowers to the girl he was with. She took one of the cookie layers and rolled it into a cone to act as a vase, thus inspiring the ice cream cone. In reality, Menches ran out of cups for the ice cream he was selling so he improvised and made his own containers by wrapping a warm thin waffle around a cone-shaped tool used for splitting thick rope.

Melon Marvels

1 (3-ounce) package lime gelatin
1 cup boiling water
1/2 cup Midori liqueur
1/2 cup vodka

Combine the gelatin and boiling water in a bowl, stirring until the gelatin dissolves. Add the liqueur and vodka and mix well. Pour into a shallow dish. Chill until set. Cut into cubes. Spoon into small glasses. Yield: 12 servings.

Bacon and Swiss Bites

1 cup shredded Swiss cheese
1 (4-ounce) can chopped black olives, drained
1/4 cup crumbled crisp-fried bacon
1/4 cup chopped green onions
1/4 cup mayonnaise
2 teaspoons Worcestershire sauce
1 (1-pound) loaf party rye or pumpernickel bread

Combine the cheese, black olives, bacon and green onions in a bowl and mix well. Stir in the mayonnaise and Worcestershire sauce.

Spread the cheese mixture over 1 side of each bread slice. Arrange the slices on an ungreased baking sheet.

Bake at 350 degrees in a preheated oven for 10 to 15 minutes or until bubbly. Yield: variable.

Churchills

6 English muffins, split
1½ cups mayonnaise
1 large onion, chopped
1 egg, beaten
1 tablespoon granulated garlic, or 1 garlic clove, crushed
1 cup grated Parmesan cheese
Paprika to taste

Arrange the muffin halves cut side up on a baking sheet. Combine the mayonnaise, onion, egg, garlic and cheese in a bowl and mix well. Spread the mixture over the muffin halves. Sprinkle with paprika.

Bake at 375 degrees in a preheated oven for 10 to 15 minutes or until light brown.

Cut each muffin half into quarters. Garnish with sprigs of fresh parsley. May toast muffins before spreading with topping.
Yield: 48 servings.

The name Akron stems from the Greek word akro, *meaning "highest point." Early land developers decided on the area as the best place for the Ohio & Erie and the Pennsylvania & Ohio canals to meet. In fact, the second highest point in the entire state of Ohio (1,100 feet), just west of the intersection of West Market Street and Portage Path, is but a few feet from the Junior League of Akron's headquarters.*

Crab Melt-a-Ways

6 English muffins, split
1 (5-ounce) jar Old English Cheddar cheese spread
1/4 cup (1/2 stick) butter or margarine, softened
2 tablespoons mayonnaise
1 teaspoon seasoned salt
1/8 teaspoon garlic powder
1 (8-ounce) can crab meat, drained

Arrange the muffin halves cut side up on a baking sheet. Combine the cheese spread, butter, mayonnaise, seasoned salt and garlic powder in a bowl and mix well. Stir in the crab meat. Spread the crab mixture over the muffin halves. Freeze for 30 minutes.

Once firm, cut each muffin half into quarters. Transfer the quarters to a freezer container. Store in the freezer until just before serving time.

Arrange the desired number of muffin quarters on a baking sheet. Broil in a preheated oven for 3 to 5 minutes or until brown and bubbly. Serve immediately. Yield: 48 servings.

Nutty Delights

1/2 cup shredded Swiss cheese
1/4 cup finely chopped walnuts
1/2 cup mayonnaise
16 slices party rye bread

Combine the cheese and walnuts in a bowl and mix well. Add the mayonnaise gradually, stirring until mixed. Spread the cheese mixture over 1 side of each bread slice. Arrange the slices on a baking sheet. Broil in a preheated oven for 5 minutes or until golden brown and bubbly. Serve immediately. Yield: 16 servings.

Pesto Toasts

1 cup pesto sauce
1 baguette French bread, cut into 1/2-inch slices
8 ounces asiago cheese, thinly sliced

Spread the pesto sauce on 1 side of each baguette slice. Arrange the slices on a baking sheet. Top with the cheese. Broil in a preheated oven just until the cheese melts, but not bubbly. Yield: 16 servings.

Basil is the Greek word for "royal" or "kingly." Ancient Greeks believed only the king himself should be allowed to harvest basil. In Italy, however, basil is considered a token of love. And in Romania, a couple is considered engaged when a boy accepts a sprig of basil from a girl.

Poor Boy Canapés

8 ounces sharp Cheddar cheese, shredded
8 ounces extra-sharp Cheddar cheese, shredded
1 (8-ounce) can tomato sauce
1/2 cup vegetable or corn oil
1/3 to 1/2 cup chopped green bell pepper, or to taste
6 green onions, chopped
1 (7-ounce) jar pimento-stuffed green olives, drained, chopped
1 baguette French bread, cut into 1/2-inch slices

Combine all the cheese, tomato sauce, oil, green pepper, green onions and green olives in a bowl and mix well. Spread the cheese mixture over 1 side of each bread slice. Arrange the slices on a baking sheet.

Bake at 350 degrees in a preheated oven until the cheese is melted but not bubbly. Serve immediately.

Add shredded ham or shredded cooked chicken to the cheese mixture for variety. May prepare the cheese mixture in advance and store, covered, in the refrigerator until just before baking. Substitute 1 small chopped yellow onion for the green onions if desired. Yield: 16 servings.

Greek Pizza

1 (12-inch) prebaked pizza crust
3/4 cup chopped tomato
1 cup shredded mozzarella cheese
1 cup crumbled feta cheese
1 small red onion, sliced
1/4 cup chopped fresh basil
1/4 cup sliced black olives
1/4 teaspoon oregano, crushed

Place the pizza crust on a baking sheet. Sprinkle with the tomato, mozzarella cheese, feta cheese, red onion, basil, black olives and oregano in the order listed.

Bake at 450 degrees in a preheated oven for 10 minutes or until bubbly. Yield: 4 to 6 servings.

Two canals passed through downtown Akron, but the growth of the local economy was due more to the "staircase locks" that lifted canal boats through the changes in elevation. Canal boats took at least six hours on a good day to pass through the series of twenty-one locks in just two miles of waterway.

Mexican Pizza Squares

2 (8-count each) cans crescent rolls
1 pound ground sirloin
1 teaspoon chili powder
3/4 cup salsa
1/3 cup sour cream
1 to 1 1/2 cups shredded Monterey Jack cheese
1 to 1 1/2 cups shredded Cheddar cheese
1 (4-ounce) can sliced black or green olives, drained
1 jar sliced jalapeño chiles, drained
1 avocado, thinly sliced (optional)

Unroll the dough. Separate into rectangles. Pat the dough over the bottom of a 10x15-inch baking sheet, pressing the edges and perforations to seal. Bake using package directions. Let stand until cool.

Brown the ground sirloin with the chili powder in a skillet, stirring until the ground sirloin is crumbly; drain. Combine the salsa and sour cream in a bowl and mix well.

Spread the salsa mixture over the baked layer. Sprinkle with the ground sirloin. Top with the Monterey Jack cheese, Cheddar cheese, black olives and chiles. Bake at 400 degrees in a preheated oven for 10 minutes or until bubbly. Cut into squares. Top each square with an avocado slice. Yield: 9 servings.

Pesto Pizza

1 cup packed fresh basil leaves
1/3 cup pine nuts or walnuts
1/3 cup grated Romano or Parmesan cheese
1/3 cup olive oil
1/4 teaspoon kosher salt
1/4 teaspoon freshly ground pepper
1 large garlic clove
1 Boboli pizza crust
8 ounces white cheese in any combination, shredded

Combine the basil, pine nuts, Romano cheese, olive oil, kosher salt, pepper and garlic in a blender container fitted with a grating or mincing blade. Process until puréed and thickened. Place the pizza crust on a pizza pan. Spread with the basil purée. Sprinkle with the white cheese.

Bake at 450 degrees in a preheated oven for 10 to 12 minutes or until bubbly. Cool slightly. Cut into 16 slices. The pesto sauce can be prepared in advance and stored, covered, in the freezer for future use. Add sun-dried tomatoes to the sauce for a unique flavor. Yield: 16 servings.

Construction of the Ohio & Erie canal began in 1825, the year Akron was founded. The canal was opened for traffic in 1827 and closed permanently in 1913 when several of the locks had to be dynamited during a disastrous flood.

Pizza Thins

1 pound bulk sausage
1 pound ground beef
1 pound Velveeta cheese, shredded
2 teaspoons Worcestershire sauce
1 teaspoon oregano
1/2 teaspoon garlic powder
2 loaves party rye bread

Brown the sausage in a skillet, stirring until crumbly; drain. Blot with paper towels to absorb the excess fat. Brown the ground beef in a skillet, stirring until crumbly; drain. Blot with paper towels to absorb the excess fat. Combine the sausage, ground beef, cheese, Worcestershire sauce, oregano and garlic powder in a skillet and mix well. Cook just until the cheese melts, stirring frequently.

Spread 1 teaspoon of the sausage mixture over each slice of bread. Arrange the slices on a baking sheet. Freeze until firm. Bake at 325 degrees in a preheated oven for 15 minutes or store in freezer bags for future use. Garnish each slice with sliced green olives and/or red or green bell pepper strips. Yield: 80 pizza thins.

Idaho Apple Dip

6 unpeeled Idaho Red Delicious or Rome apples
Lemon juice to taste
8 ounces cream cheese, softened
3 tablespoons whipping cream
4 ounces bleu cheese, crumbled

Core the apples and cut into bite-size pieces. Insert wooden picks into the apple pieces and dip in lemon juice. Insert the opposite end of the wooden pick in a whole apple.

Beat the cream cheese and whipping cream in a mixing bowl until blended. Add the bleu cheese and beat until smooth. Spoon into a serving bowl. Serve with the apples. Yield: 24 servings.

Today, parts of the original canals are being restored for recreational use. In the Cuyahoga Valley National Recreation Area—a 33,000-acre national park between Akron and Cleveland—a bike path along the water loosely traces the former towpath used by horses and mules as they pulled the boats along the canal and its locks.

Dewey Beach Bean Dip

1 (16-ounce) can refried beans
1 envelope taco seasoning mix
1 cup sour cream
1 (16-ounce) can black olives, drained, chopped
6 to 8 scallions or green onions, chopped
3 or 4 tomatoes, chopped
8 ounces Cheddar cheese, shredded
8 ounces Monterey Jack cheese, shredded
Corn chips

Combine the refried beans and seasoning mix in a bowl and mix well. Spread in a 9x13-inch baking pan.

Layer the sour cream, black olives, scallions, tomatoes, Cheddar cheese and Monterey Jack cheese over the beans in the order listed.

Bake at 350 degrees in a preheated oven for 30 minutes or until bubbly. Serve with corn chips. Yield: 6 to 8 servings.

Outlaw Salsa

2 large tomatoes, seeded, chopped
1/4 cup chopped red onion
1/4 cup chopped fresh cilantro
1 avocado, chopped
2 (15 ounces each) cans black beans, drained
1 (15-ounce) can whole kernel corn, drained
3 tablespoons fresh lime juice
2 tablespoons extra-virgin olive oil
1 tablespoon red wine vinegar
Salt and pepper to taste
Blue and white tortilla chips

Combine the tomatoes, red onion, 1/4 cup cilantro and avocado in a bowl and mix gently. Stir in the beans and corn.

Whisk the lime juice, olive oil, wine vinegar, salt and pepper in a bowl until blended. Pour over the tomato mixture and toss gently to coat.

Garnish with sprigs of cilantro. Serve with tortilla chips.
Yield: 15 to 20 servings.

Schools in Akron were the first to unite in a "public school system," joined and organized under one political body, or "school board." In 1847, Henry King of Akron wrote the "Akron School Law," which defined public education as we know it today.

Black Bean Salsa

2 cups canned black beans, cooked, drained
1/2 cup canned corn
1 avocado, chopped
1/2 cup chopped red bell pepper
1/2 cup chopped red onion
1 or 2 jalapeño chiles, seeded, chopped
2 to 3 tablespoons extra-virgin olive oil
1/2 cup finely chopped fresh cilantro
3 to 4 tablespoons lime juice, or to taste
Salt and pepper to taste
Blue tortilla chips or toasted pita wedges

Combine the beans, corn, avocado, red pepper, onion, jalapeños, olive oil and cilantro in a bowl and mix well. Stir in the lime juice. Season with salt and pepper. Serve with tortilla chips or pita wedges. Yield: 6 to 8 servings.

Bleu Cheese Dip

4 ounces cream cheese, softened
1/2 cup crumbled bleu cheese
2 tablespoons whole or 2% milk
1 tablespoon port
2 sprigs of fresh parsley, stems removed
Fresh vegetables or assorted party crackers

Combine the cream cheese, bleu cheese, milk, wine and parsley in a blender container. Process until smooth. Spoon into a serving bowl. Serve with fresh vegetables or assorted party crackers. Yield: 1 cup.

Broccoli Dip

2 (10 ounces each) packages frozen chopped broccoli
1 cup chopped onion
¼ cup (½ stick) margarine
1 (10-ounce) can cream of mushroom soup
1 cup shredded Cheddar cheese
1 (4-ounce) jar sliced mushrooms, drained
½ teaspoon garlic powder
Corn chips

Cook the broccoli using package directions; drain. Sauté the onion in the margarine in a skillet until tender. Stir in the soup, cheese, mushrooms and garlic powder. Add a small amount of milk if needed for the desired consistency. Spoon into a baking dish.

Bake at 350 degrees in a preheated oven for 30 minutes or until bubbly. Serve with corn chips. Yield: 12 to 15 servings.

Charles E. Menches is credited as the inventor of the hamburger. At the 1885 Erie County Fair in Hamburg, New York, he ran out of sausage at his booth, so he bought five pounds of beef, chopped it into small pieces, and seasoned it with brown sugar, salt, pepper, and coffee. It was a tremendous success, and hamburgers made from the original recipe are still being served at the Menches Brothers Family Restaurants in the Akron area.

Chili Dip, Cincinnati-Style

8 ounces cream cheese, softened
1 small onion, chopped
Cincinnati-Style Chili (below)
2 cups shredded Cheddar cheese
Tortilla chips

Spread the cream cheese to measure 1/4 to 1/2 inch over the bottom of an 8x8-inch or 9x9-inch microwave-safe dish. Sprinkle with the onion. Spread with enough chili to measure 1/4 to 1/2 inch. Top with the Cheddar cheese. Microwave for 3 minutes or until bubbly and heated through. Serve with tortilla chips. Yield: 12 servings.

Cincinnati-Style Chili

2 pounds ground beef
7 cups water
1 (12-ounce) can tomato paste
3 tablespoons dried onion
1 tablespoon chili powder
1 tablespoon salt
1 tablespoon Worcestershire sauce
1 tablespoon vinegar
1 teaspoon cinnamon
1 teaspoon cumin
1 teaspoon chopped red chiles
1 teaspoon allspice
1/2 teaspoon garlic powder
4 bay leaves

Combine the ground beef and water in a saucepan and mix well. Stir in the tomato paste, dried onion, chili powder, salt, Worcestershire sauce, vinegar, cinnamon, cumin, chiles, allspice, garlic powder and bay leaves. Bring to a boil; reduce heat. Simmer for 4 hours, stirring occasionally. Discard the bay leaves.
Yield: 6 to 8 servings.

Dill Dip in a Bread Bowl

2 large round loaves Russian or pumpernickel bread
2²/₃ cups sour cream
2²/₃ cups mayonnaise
¼ cup finely chopped fresh parsley
¼ cup grated onion
6 teaspoons chopped fresh dillweed, or 4 teaspoons dried dillweed
4 teaspoons Beau Monde seasoning

Cut a circle from the center of each loaf with a serrated knife to form a bowl, leaving the sides intact. Cut the bread from the center into cubes. Cut the second loaf into cubes. Set aside.

Combine the sour cream, mayonnaise, parsley, onion, dillweed and Beau Monde seasoning in a bowl and mix well. Spoon into the bread bowl.

Arrange the bread bowl on a serving platter. Surround the bowl with the bread cubes and/or fresh vegetables.

May substitute light sour cream for the sour cream. Do not use nonfat sour cream. Chill the dip for 8 to 10 hours before serving if using dried dillweed. Yield: 30 servings.

The Akron school system was among the first in the nation to be publicly financed. Before that, schools received funding through churches or by other means.

Italian Eggplant Dip

2 tablespoons extra-virgin olive oil
Minced garlic to taste
1 large eggplant
1 small red onion, chopped
1 large tomato, chopped
¼ cup Italian-seasoned bread crumbs
¼ cup seasoned vinegar
2 tablespoons chopped fresh parsley
¼ teaspoon hot pepper sauce
Pita chips

Combine the olive oil and garlic in a bowl and mix well. Pierce the eggplant several times with a fork. Microwave on High for 10 minutes. Let stand until cool. Cut the eggplant into halves. Scoop out the pulp and coarsely chop.

Stir the eggplant into the garlic mixture. Add the onion, tomato, bread crumbs, vinegar, parsley and hot pepper sauce and mix well. Garnish with sprigs of fresh parsley. Serve with pita chips.
Yield: 8 to 10 servings.

Ginger and Lime Fruit Dip

1/2 cup mayonnaise
1/2 cup sour cream
2 tablespoons fresh lime juice
2 tablespoons honey
1 tablespoon minced crystallized ginger
1 1/2 teaspoons grated lime zest
Assorted fresh fruit

Combine the mayonnaise, sour cream, lime juice, honey, ginger
and lime zest in a bowl and mix well. Serve with assorted fresh
fruits. May add several drops of green food coloring if desired.
Yield: 8 servings.

Photograph for this recipe appears on the cover.

Green Goddess Dip

1 cup mayonnaise
1/2 cup sour cream
1/3 cup chopped fresh parsley
1 (2-ounce) can anchovies, drained, chopped
3 tablespoons chopped fresh chives
1 tablespoon vinegar
1 garlic clove, crushed or minced
Assorted fresh vegetables

Combine the mayonnaise, sour cream, parsley, anchovies, chives,
vinegar and garlic in a bowl and mix well. Add a small amount of
milk if desired for a thinner consistency. Chill, covered, for 8 to
10 hours. Serve with assorted fresh vegetables. May substitute
3 tablespoons parsley flakes for the fresh parsley and 1 tablespoon
dried chives for the fresh chives. Yield: 12 to 15 servings.

*"The world is round and
the place which may seem
like the end may also be
only the beginning."*

—Ivy Baker Priest, 1958

Light Guacamole

1 ripe avocado
2 tablespoons fresh lime juice
1/2 cup plain nonfat yogurt
1 tablespoon minced red onion
1/4 teaspoon salt
1/4 teaspoon ground red pepper
1/8 teaspoon cumin
Tortilla chips

Mash the avocado with the lime juice in a bowl. Stir in the yogurt, onion, salt, red pepper and cumin. Serve with tortilla chips.
Yield: 1 1/2 cups.

Horseradish Chip Dip

8 ounces cream cheese, softened
2 to 4 tablespoons milk
3 tablespoons sour cream
2 tablespoons prepared horseradish
2 tablespoons mayonnaise
1 teaspoon Worcestershire sauce
1/2 teaspoon onion salt
1/2 teaspoon garlic salt
Corn chips

Beat the cream cheese and milk in a mixing bowl until smooth, scraping the bowl occasionally. Add the sour cream, horseradish, mayonnaise, Worcestershire sauce, onion salt and garlic salt 1 at a time, mixing well after each addition. Spoon into a serving bowl. Chill, covered, for several hours before serving. Serve with corn chips or assorted fresh vegetables. Yield: 8 to 10 servings.

Mississippi Sin

1 round loaf French or rye bread
8 ounces cream cheese, softened
2 cups shredded Cheddar cheese
1 1/2 cups sour cream
1/2 cup chopped ham
1/3 cup chopped green chiles
1/3 cup chopped green onions

Remove the center of the loaf carefully, leaving the side intact to form a shell. Cut the bread from the center into cubes.

Beat the cream cheese, Cheddar cheese and sour cream in a mixing bowl until blended. Stir in the ham, chiles and green onions. Spoon into the bread shell.

Wrap the bread shell in foil. Bake at 350 degrees in a preheated oven for 1 hour. Serve with the bread cubes and/or assorted party crackers. Yield: 15 to 20 servings.

The late John S. Knight, legendary newspaper baron, got his start in Akron. This Pulitzer Prize-winning editor was founder and principal owner of the Knight-Ridder Newspapers, a national chain of newspapers that includes the Akron Beacon Journal.

Awesome Party Nacho Dip

1 pound Velveeta cheese, cut into 1-inch cubes
1 (12-ounce) can tomatoes with green chiles, chopped
1 (4-ounce) can chopped green chiles
1/4 teaspoon Tabasco sauce, or to taste
Corn chips or tortilla chips

Combine the cheese, undrained tomatoes and undrained chiles
in a microwave-safe dish. Microwave on High for 5 minutes; stir.
Microwave for 3 to 5 minutes longer or until the cheese melts;
stir. Add the Tabasco sauce and mix well. Spoon the dip into a
serving bowl. Serve with corn chips and/or tortilla chips.

For a different twist on serving, spoon the nacho dip into a shallow
serving bowl and top with a dollop of sour cream. Border the dip
with your favorite salsa. Yield: 8 to 12 servings.

Hot Cheese Dip

12 ounces Monterey Jack cheese, shredded
1 (4-ounce) can chopped green chiles
1 egg, beaten
Tortilla chips or corn chips

Combine the cheese, undrained chiles and egg in a bowl and mix
well. Spoon into a 9x9-inch baking dish. Bake at 350 degrees in a
preheated oven until heated through; do not overbake. Serve with
tortilla chips and/or corn chips. Yield: 12 servings.

Nine-Layer Tex-Mex Dip

1 (12-ounce) can bean dip
3 avocados, mashed
1 tablespoon lemon juice
3 tablespoons mayonnaise
1/2 envelope taco seasoning mix
1/2 cup shredded Monterey Jack cheese
1 cup chopped green onions
1/2 cup chopped fresh parsley or cilantro
3 medium tomatoes, chopped
1 cup sliced black or green olives
1/2 cup shredded Cheddar cheese
Tortilla chips

Spread the bean dip over the bottom of a shallow 2-quart dish. Combine the avocados and lemon juice in a bowl and mix well. Spread over the bean dip. Combine the mayonnaise and seasoning mix in a bowl and mix well. Spread over the prepared layers.

Layer the Monterey Jack cheese, green onions, parsley, tomatoes, black olives and Cheddar cheese in the order listed over the prepared layers. Serve with tortilla chips. Vary layers and amounts of ingredients according to taste and preference. Yield: 30 servings.

The first cookbook written by an American, American Cookery *by Amelia Simmons, was published in 1796. It helped begin a vogue for printing cookbooks by Americans, mostly women. Today, the cookbook ranks as the third most important and most often consulted book in the household, surpassed only by the Bible and telephone directory.*

Peanut Butter Apple Dip

8 ounces cream cheese, softened
1 cup peanut butter
1 cup packed brown sugar
1/4 cup milk
Red and green apple wedges

Combine the cream cheese, peanut butter, brown sugar and milk in a mixing bowl. Beat until smooth, scraping the bowl occasionally. Spoon into a serving bowl. Serve with apple wedges. Store the leftover dip in the refrigerator. Yield: 2²/₃ cups.

Raspberry Cream Fruit Dip

6 ounces cream cheese, softened
1 tablespoon brown sugar
1 tablespoon red wine vinegar
1/2 teaspoon ground ginger
1 cup raspberries, crushed
Assorted fresh fruit

Beat the cream cheese, brown sugar, wine vinegar and ginger in a mixing bowl until blended, scraping the bowl occasionally. Stir in the raspberries. Spoon into a serving bowl. Chill, covered, until serving time. Serve with fresh fruit. Yield: 1¹/₄ cups.

Photograph for this recipe appears on the cover.

Hot Reuben Dip

1 (14-ounce) can sauerkraut, drained
4 ounces cooked corned beef
1 small onion, finely chopped
1 cup mayonnaise
1 cup sour cream
1 cup shredded Swiss cheese
2 tablespoons prepared horseradish
1 teaspoon Dijon mustard (optional)
Party rye bread

Squeeze the excess moisture from the sauerkraut. Process the sauerkraut, corned beef and onion in a blender or food processor fitted with a steel blade until finely chopped. Combine the corned beef mixture, mayonnaise, sour cream, cheese, horseradish and Dijon mustard in a bowl and mix well.

Spoon the corned beef mixture into a 1-quart baking dish sprayed with nonstick cooking spray. Bake at 350 degrees in a preheated oven for 30 to 40 minutes or until bubbly. Serve with party rye bread. May use reduced-fat mayonnaise and reduced-fat sour cream. Yield: 5 cups.

The mass-production toy industry began in Akron. In 1888, Samuel Dyke of S.C. Dyke & Co. began making marbles and became the nation's first toy maker. Before then, most toys were imported from Germany and only the very wealthy could afford them. But Dyke thought that if marbles could be mass-produced, all children could afford to buy them—pioneering the concept of children as consumers. At the turn of the last century, Akron was the "Marble Capital of the World," with 25 different marble companies shipping over one million marbles each day.

Shrimp Dip

2 cups sour cream
6 ounces cream cheese, softened
1 cup finely chopped cooked shrimp
¼ cup chopped green bell pepper (optional)
1 envelope Italian salad dressing mix
4 teaspoons lemon juice
Assorted crackers or assorted fresh vegetables

Beat the sour cream and cream cheese in a mixing bowl until smooth, scraping the bowl occasionally. Stir in the shrimp, green pepper, dressing mix and lemon juice.

Chill, covered, for 1 hour or longer. Serve with assorted party crackers or fresh vegetables. Yield: 25 servings.

Swiss Dip

1 cup shredded Swiss cheese
1 cup mayonnaise
1/2 cup finely minced onion
Wheat crackers

Combine the cheese, mayonnaise and onion in a bowl and mix
well. Spoon into a 3-cup baking dish. Bake at 350 degrees in a
preheated oven for 30 minutes. Serve with wheat crackers. May
substitute reduced-fat mayonnaise for the mayonnaise.
Yield: 6 to 8 servings.

Swiss Almond Dip

8 ounces cream cheese, softened
1 1/2 cups shredded Swiss cheese
1/3 cup mayonnaise-type salad dressing
1/3 cup sliced almonds, toasted
2 tablespoons chopped green onions
1/8 teaspoon nutmeg
1/8 teaspoon pepper
Assorted party crackers or pita chips

Beat the cream cheese, Swiss cheese and salad dressing in a mixing
bowl until blended. Stir in the almonds, green onions, nutmeg
and pepper. Spoon into a round baking dish. Bake at 350 degrees
in a preheated oven for 8 minutes; stir. Bake for 7 minutes longer.
Sprinkle with additional toasted almonds. Serve warm with
assorted party crackers or pita chips. Yield: 10 to 12 servings.

*Akron was once the home
of a minor league team for
the New York Yankees.
In 1997, minor league
baseball returned to Akron
in the form of the Akron
Aeros in their beautiful
new stadium "Canal
Park." The Aeros are
affiliated with the
Cleveland Indians.*

Vidalia Onion Dip

2 cups chopped Vidalia onions
2 cups shredded Jarlsberg cheese
2 cups mayonnaise
Assorted party crackers or party bread

Combine the onions, cheese and mayonnaise in a bowl and mix
well. Spoon into a 9x13-inch baking dish. Bake at 350 degrees in
a preheated oven for 30 minutes. Serve warm with assorted party
crackers or party bread. Yield: 6 to 8 servings.

Appetizer Pie

8 ounces cream cheese, softened
1/2 cup sour cream
2 tablespoons milk
1 (2-ounce) package dried beef, chopped
2 tablespoons instant minced onion
2 tablespoons chopped green bell pepper
2 tablespoons chopped nuts
Pepper to taste
Assorted party crackers

Beat the cream cheese, sour cream and milk in a mixing bowl
until smooth. Stir in the dried beef, onion, green pepper, nuts
and pepper. Spoon into a baking dish. Bake at 350 degrees in a
preheated oven for 15 minutes. Serve with assorted party crackers.
Yield: 12 servings.

Derby Dried Beef Spread

16 ounces cream cheese, softened
2 (2 ounces each) packages dried beef, chopped
3/4 cup sliced green olives
1 bunch green onions, chopped
1/2 teaspoon Worcestershire sauce
1/4 teaspoon Accent seasoning
Assorted party crackers

Beat the cream cheese in a mixing bowl until smooth, scraping the bowl occasionally. Stir in the dried beef, green olives, green onions, Worcestershire sauce and Accent. Spoon into a serving bowl. Serve with assorted party crackers. Yield: 20 servings.

Layered Crab Spread

8 ounces cream cheese, softened
1 tablespoon grated onion
1 tablespoon Worcestershire sauce
1 1/2 teaspoons lemon juice
1/2 cup chili sauce
8 ounces crab meat
Hot sauce to taste
2 tablespoons chopped fresh parsley
Assorted party crackers

Beat the cream cheese in a mixing bowl until smooth. Stir in the onion, Worcestershire sauce and lemon juice. Spread the cream cheese mixture in a shallow serving dish. Spread with the chili sauce. Top with the crab meat. Sprinkle with hot sauce and parsley. Serve with assorted party crackers.
Yield: 10 to 12 servings.

"Let us watch our beginnings, and {the} results will manage themselves."

—Alexander Clark

Hot Cheese Spread

8 ounces Cheddar cheese, shredded
8 ounces Swiss cheese, shredded
1/2 medium red onion, chopped
1/2 cup mayonnaise
1 envelope onion soup mix
Assorted party crackers

Combine the Cheddar cheese, Swiss cheese and onion in a bowl and mix well. Stir in the mayonnaise. Spoon the cheese mixture into a 9x9-inch baking dish. Sprinkle with the soup mix. Bake at 300 degrees in a preheated oven for 20 minutes or until bubbly. Serve warm with assorted party crackers. Yield: 12 servings.

Mexican Snappy Appy

8 ounces cream cheese, softened
1/2 cup sour cream
2 tablespoons cumin, or to taste
1 cup salsa
1 pound deveined peeled cooked shrimp
Chopped fresh cilantro
Tortilla chips

Beat the cream cheese and sour cream in a mixing bowl until blended. Spread the cream cheese mixture over the bottom of a round dish. Sprinkle with the cumin and spread with the salsa. Top with the shrimp and cilantro. Serve with tortilla chips. Yield: 10 to 12 servings.

Pineapple Cracker Spread

16 ounces cream cheese, softened
1 (16-ounce) can crushed pineapple, drained
1 scallion or green onion, chopped
1/2 to 1 green bell pepper, chopped
Assorted party crackers

Beat the cream cheese in a mixing bowl until smooth, scraping the bowl occasionally. Stir in the pineapple, scallion and green pepper. Spoon into a serving bowl. Serve with assorted party crackers. Yield: 20 servings.

Shrimp Butter

8 ounces cream cheese, softened
1/4 cup (1/2 stick) butter, softened
4 teaspoons mayonnaise
1 (8-ounce) can shrimp, rinsed, drained, chopped
1/2 small onion, minced
Juice of 1/2 lemon
1/8 teaspoon salt
1/8 teaspoon pepper
Assorted party crackers or party bread

Beat the cream cheese, butter and mayonnaise in a mixing bowl until blended. Add the shrimp, onion, lemon juice, salt and pepper and mix well. Spoon into a serving bowl. Garnish with additional shrimp and/or sprigs of fresh parsley. Serve with assorted party crackers or party bread. Yield: 10 to 12 servings.

Shrimp Spread

1 envelope unflavored gelatin
¼ cup cold water
1 (10-ounce) can tomato soup
1 ounce cream cheese
2 (6 ounces each) cans small shrimp, drained
1 cup mayonnaise
1¼ cups chopped celery
½ cup chopped green onions
¼ cup chopped green bell pepper
Assorted party crackers or toast points

Combine the gelatin and cold water in a bowl and mix well. Let stand until softened. Combine the soup and cream cheese in a saucepan. Cook over low heat until blended, stirring frequently. Stir in the gelatin mixture. Add the shrimp, mayonnaise, celery, green onions and green pepper and mix well.

Spoon the shrimp mixture into a mold. Chill for 8 to 10 hours or until set. Invert onto a serving platter. Garnish with sprigs of fresh parsley. Serve with assorted party crackers or toast points.
Yield: 12 servings.

Spicy Shrimp Spread

3 ounces cream cheese, softened
½ cup mayonnaise
5 drops of hot pepper sauce
1 teaspoon lemon juice
1 package frozen shrimp, thawed, cooked, chopped
1 tablespoon minced fresh parsley
1 tablespoon minced green bell pepper
1 tablespoon minced onion
Assorted party crackers

Beat the cream cheese and mayonnaise in a mixing bowl until blended. Stir in the hot pepper sauce, lemon juice, shrimp, parsley, green pepper and onion. Spoon into a serving bowl. Chill, covered, until serving time. Serve with assorted party crackers. Yield: 8 to 10 servings.

A 1968 national survey showed that Akron ladies, with an average shoe size of 9C, had the biggest feet in the nation, squeezing out the women of Birmingham, Alabama, who measured in at 9B. The national average was 8C.

Strawberry Spread

6 ounces cream cheese, softened
1 cup chopped fresh or frozen strawberries
1/3 cup finely chopped pecans
2 tablespoons honey
1/4 teaspoon ginger powder
Butter crackers, party wheat bread or nut bread

Beat the cream cheese in a mixing bowl until fluffy. Add the strawberries, pecans, honey and ginger powder and mix well. Chill, covered, for 8 to 10 hours. Spoon into a serving bowl. Serve with butter crackers, party wheat bread or nut bread. Add 1 tablespoon milk to cream cheese mixture and serve as a dip with assorted fresh fruits. Yield: 10 servings.

Christmas Grapes

10 ounces pecans
8 ounces cream cheese, softened
2 ounces bleu cheese, crumbled
2 tablespoons whipping cream
1 pound seedless green and red grapes

Spread the pecans on a baking sheet. Toast at 275 degrees in a preheated oven until light brown. Let stand until cool. Chop the pecans.

Beat the cream cheese, bleu cheese and whipping cream in a mixing bowl until smooth. Press a small amount of the cream cheese mixture around each grape, enclosing completely.

Roll the grapes in the pecans. Chill, covered, until serving time. Yield: 10 servings.

Pesto and Orzo-Stuffed Cherry Tomatoes

25 cherry tomatoes
Salt to taste
1/3 cup orzo
1/3 cup pesto

Cut a thin slice from the bottom of each tomato. Slice the top off the tomatoes. Scoop out the pulp with a melon baller. Sprinkle the inside of the tomato cavities lightly with salt. Invert on paper towels. Drain for 30 minutes.

Cook the pasta using package directions until al dente. Drain and rinse with cold water; drain. Combine the pasta and pesto in a bowl and mix gently. Spoon the pesto mixture into the tomatoes. May substitute spinach dip for the pesto and orzo mixture.
Yield: 25 servings.

Photograph for this recipe appears on the cover.

Akron has twice been recognized nationally as an "All-America City," first in 1981 and again in 1995. Many years earlier, in the 1910s and 1920s, Akron was the fastest-growing city in America. From 1910 to 1920, the population grew from 69,000 to 210,000, topping off in the 300,000s in the mid-1920s.

Regas Olives

8 ounces pitted Greek olives (40 to 50 olives)
4 ounces Danish bleu cheese

Stuff each olive with an ½-inch chunk of the bleu cheese. Serve chilled or at room temperature. Yield: 40 to 50 servings.

Hamapatillas

16 ounces cream cheese or Neufchâtel cheese, softened
⅓ cup mayonnaise
2 tablespoons chopped green onions
¼ cup chopped black olives
1 package regular or super size tortillas
2 (2 ounces each) packages sliced cooked ham

Beat the cream cheese and mayonnaise in a mixing bowl until smooth, scraping the bowl occasionally. Stir in the green onions and black olives. Spread a thin layer of the cream cheese mixture on each tortilla. Arrange 2 slices of the ham on each tortilla. Roll tightly to enclose the filling.

Wrap each roll separately in plastic wrap. Chill for 3 to 10 hours. Cut each tortilla roll into ½-inch slices. Serve immediately. The flavor is enhanced if allowed to chill overnight. Yield: 40 servings.

Mexican Roll-Ups

16 ounces cream cheese, softened
1 envelope ranch salad dressing mix
1 (4-ounce) jar pimentos, drained, chopped
1 (4-ounce) can chopped green chiles, drained
1 (4-ounce) can chopped black olives, drained
10 (10-inch) flour tortillas

Beat the cream cheese and dressing mix in a mixing bowl until blended, scraping the bowl occasionally. Combine the pimentos, chiles and black olives in a bowl and mix well.

Spread a thin layer of the cream cheese mixture on each tortilla. Sprinkle with the pimento mixture. Roll tightly to enclose the filling.

Wrap each roll in plastic wrap. Chill for 2 to 10 hours. Cut each roll into 1/2-inch slices. Serve with salsa if desired.
Yield: 40 servings.

The first automobile police patrol wagon in the country was designed by electrician Frank Fowler Loomis of Akron. It was placed in service in June 1899 by the Akron Police Department. This electrically powered vehicle had three speeds, the fastest being 16 miles per hour. When not loaded with criminals, it weighed 5,500 pounds (including the battery).

Veggie Roll-Ups

8 ounces cream cheese, softened
1 envelope ranch salad dressing mix
10 (10-inch) flour tortillas
8 ounces mushrooms, finely chopped
1 (4-ounce) can chopped black olives, drained
1 rib celery, finely chopped
1 green bell pepper, finely chopped
1 red bell pepper, finely chopped
1 bunch green onions, finely sliced
1 cup shredded Cheddar cheese

Beat the cream cheese and salad dressing mix in a mixing bowl until smooth. Spread a thin layer of the cream cheese mixture on each tortilla. Sprinkle with the mushrooms, black olives, celery, green pepper, red pepper, green onions and Cheddar cheese. Roll tightly to enclose the filling.

Wrap each tortilla roll separately in plastic wrap. Chill for 8 to 10 hours. Cut each roll into 1/2-inch slices. Yield: 40 servings.

Bacon Bites

1 pound bacon
60 club crackers
Garlic powder or garlic salt to taste
Kosher salt to taste

Cut each bacon slice into thirds. Wrap the bacon around the crackers. Arrange the crackers seam side down on a broiler rack. Sprinkle with garlic powder and kosher salt. Bake at 300 degrees in a preheated oven for 30 minutes. Let stand until cool.

For variety, mix 1/3 cup packed brown sugar and 2 tablespoons chili powder. Spoon 1/2 teaspoon of the mixture over each wrapped cracker before baking. Yield: 10 to 15 servings.

Bacon-Wrapped Breadsticks

1 cup packed brown sugar
6 tablespoons chili powder
30 slices bacon
60 very thin breadsticks

Combine the brown sugar and chili powder in a bowl and mix well. Spread on a baking sheet. Cut the bacon lengthwise to make 60 strips. Wrap 1 strip of the bacon around each breadstick to cover the length. Roll in the brown sugar mixture.

Arrange the breadsticks on a broiler rack in a broiler pan. Bake at 350 degrees in a preheated oven for 20 minutes. Loosen the breadsticks with a spatula. Let stand for 15 minutes. Serve at room temperature. Yield: 60 breadsticks.

Nicknamed "The Rubber City," Akron led the country in tire manufacturing and innovation. It was the hometown to the headquarters of most of the largest rubber manufacturers in the nation.

Bacon and Cream Cheese Crisps

8 ounces cream cheese, softened
8 slices crisp-fried bacon, crumbled
1/3 cup grated Parmesan cheese
1/4 cup finely chopped onion
2 tablespoons chopped fresh parsley
1 tablespoon milk
2 (8-count each) cans crescent rolls
1 egg, beaten
1 teaspoon cold water
Poppy seeds to taste

Combine the cream cheese, bacon, Parmesan cheese, onion, parsley and milk in a mixing bowl. Beat at medium speed until mixed, scraping the bowl occasionally.

Separate the roll dough into 8 rectangles, pressing perforations to seal. Spread 2 tablespoons of the cream cheese mixture over each rectangle. Fold over to enclose the filling. Cut each rectangle into 4 or 5 slices. Arrange the slices on a greased baking sheet.

Brush each slice with a mixture of the egg and cold water. Sprinkle with poppy seeds. Bake at 375 degrees in a preheated oven for 12 to 15 minutes or until golden brown. Yield: 40 crisps.

Cheese Bake

2½ cups baking mix
1½ cups milk
2 eggs
1 pound Cheddar cheese, shredded
1 pound Monterey Jack cheese, shredded

Combine the baking mix, milk and eggs in a bowl and mix well.
Stir in the Cheddar cheese and Monterey Jack cheese. Spoon into
a 9x13-inch baking pan. Bake at 325 degrees in a preheated
oven for 30 minutes. Turn off the oven. Let stand in oven for
5 minutes. Remove from oven. Let stand until cool. Cut into
squares in pan. Bake at 400 degrees in a preheated oven for 10 to
15 minutes. Yield: 36 squares.

Cheese Puffs

1 cup water
½ cup (1 stick) butter
½ cup flour
½ cup shredded Cheddar cheese
2 eggs

Bring the water to a boil in a saucepan. Add the butter, stirring
until melted. Stir in the flour and cheese. Cook for 3 minutes,
stirring frequently. Let stand until cool. Add the eggs 1 at a time,
beating well after each addition.

Drop the batter by small teaspoonfuls onto a greased baking
sheet. Bake at 400 degrees in a preheated oven for 20 minutes.
Serve immediately. Yield: 60 puffs.

Matchbooks originated in the Akron area. These "safety matches" were first manufactured in 1896 by the Diamond Match Co. at its Barberton factory. In the 1870s and 1880s, O.C. Barber and his match empire had a virtual monopoly nationally on the production of matches.

Party Cheese Puffs

1 loaf French bread
2 cups shredded sharp Cheddar cheese
1 cup heavy cream
$1/2$ cup (1 stick) butter, softened
$1/8$ teaspoon cayenne pepper

Freeze the bread for 1 hour or until firm. Trim the crust. Cut the bread into $1^{1/2}$-inch cubes. Combine the cheese, heavy cream, butter and cayenne pepper in a double boiler.

Cook over simmering water for 5 to 10 minutes or until blended, stirring constantly. Spear the bread cubes with a fork and swirl in the cheese mixture until coated. Transfer the bread cubes to a baking sheet lined with waxed paper. Freeze for 1 hour.

Arrange the bread cubes on a baking sheet. Bake at 450 degrees in a preheated oven for 5 to 10 minutes or until light brown and heated through. Yield: 15 servings.

Curried Cheese Puffs

2 teaspoons curry powder
$\frac{1}{2}$ teaspoon coriander
$\frac{1}{2}$ teaspoon cumin
$\frac{1}{4}$ teaspoon cayenne pepper
1 cup water
6 tablespoons butter
$\frac{1}{2}$ teaspoon salt
1 cup flour
4 eggs, beaten
1 cup shredded Cheddar cheese

Combine the curry powder, coriander, cumin and cayenne pepper in a saucepan. Cook over medium heat for 1 minute, stirring constantly. Add the water, butter and salt and mix well. Bring to a boil over high heat. Reduce heat to medium-low.

Stir in the flour. Cook until the mixture forms a ball, stirring constantly. Remove from heat. Stir in the eggs. Beat until the batter is smooth and satiny. Stir in the cheese.

Drop by teaspoonfuls or pipe into small mounds 1 inch apart onto a baking sheet. Bake at 400 degrees in a preheated oven for 25 to 30 minutes or until golden brown, rotating baking sheet as needed. May freeze for future use. Yield: 20 servings.

"The beginning is the most important part of the work."
—*Plato*

Cheese Straws

1 pound New York Cheddar cheese
1/2 cup unsalted butter
1/4 cup margarine
2 cups unbleached or white flour
1 1/2 teaspoons cayenne pepper
1/4 teaspoon salt

Shred the cheese in a food processor fitted with a medium grating blade. Remove the grating blade and fit the processor with a metal blade. Add the butter and margarine to the food processor container. Process until creamy, scraping the side occasionally.

Combine the flour, cayenne pepper and salt in a bowl and mix well. Add the flour mixture 1/2 cup at a time to the cheese mixture, processing constantly until combined. Spoon into a pastry bag fitted with a star or ribbon tip. Pipe into strips onto an ungreased baking sheet. Bake at 300 degrees in a preheated oven for 15 to 20 minutes or until light brown; do not overbake. Let stand until cool. Break into desired lengths. Yield: 100 servings.

Pepper Cheese Crisps

4 cups shredded pepper Jack cheese
2 cups flour
2 cups crisp rice cereal
2 teaspoons sugar
1/2 teaspoon salt
1/2 teaspoon dry mustard
1/8 to 1/4 teaspoon Worcestershire sauce
1/8 teaspoon cayenne pepper (optional)
1 cup (2 sticks) butter, melted

Combine the cheese, flour, cereal, sugar, salt, dry mustard, Worcestershire sauce and cayenne pepper in a bowl and mix well. Add the butter and mix well. Shape into 1-inch balls.

Arrange the balls 1 inch apart on a baking sheet. Press each ball into a 3/8-inch-thick circle with a fork. Bake at 350 degrees in a preheated oven for 10 to 12 minutes or until brown. Serve warm or at room temperature. Yield: 15 servings.

The oldest house still standing in Ohio is found in the Akron area. Located in Hudson, Ohio, and built in 1805, it was once the residence of Deacon David Hudson, who in 1800 settled the area that bears his name.

Spicy Cheese Crackers

2 cups shredded Cheddar cheese, softened
1/2 cup (1 stick) butter, softened
1 1/2 cups flour
1/2 teaspoon salt
1/4 teaspoon ground red pepper

Combine the cheese and butter in a mixing bowl. Beat until blended, scraping the bowl occasionally. Add the flour, salt and red pepper, stirring until of a dough consistency.

Divide the dough into 2 equal portions. Shape each portion into a 7- or 8-inch log. Wrap each log in plastic wrap. Chill for 1 hour.

Cut each log into 1/4-inch slices with a sharp knife or crinkle cutter. Arrange on an ungreased baking sheet. Bake at 350 degrees in a preheated oven for 15 minutes. Yield: 24 servings.

Spicy Cheese Sticks

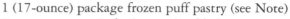

1 (17-ounce) package frozen puff pastry (see Note)
8 ounces pepper Jack cheese, shredded
1 teaspoon chili powder
1 teaspoon salt
1 egg, beaten

The modern golf ball was born in Akron. Corburn Haskell of Cleveland came to Akron in 1899 for a golf date with B.F. Goodrich superintendent B.G. Work. While waiting for Work at the plant, Haskell idly wound a long rubber thread into a ball. When he bounced it, it flew almost to the ceiling. "Now, there's a golf ball," he joked. "Maybe," Work said, "if we put a cover on it." Before that time, players had used a solid white rubber ball.

Thaw the puff pastry using package directions. Roll 1 sheet of the pastry into a 15x15-inch square on a lightly floured surface with a floured rolling pin. Cut the square into halves. Sprinkle half the cheese on 1 pastry half. Top with the remaining pastry half. Roll into a 10x15-inch rectangle. Sprinkle with 1/2 teaspoon of the chili powder and 1/2 teaspoon of the salt and press gently with the rolling pin. Turn the pastry rectangle over and brush with half the egg. Cut crosswise into twenty 3/4x10-inch strips.

Twist each pastry strip several times. Arrange 1/2 inch apart on a greased baking sheet. Bake at 375 degrees in a preheated oven for 15 to 20 minutes or until brown and crisp. Remove to a wire rack to cool. Repeat the procedure with the remaining pastry, cheese, chili powder, salt and egg. Store the cheese sticks in a loosely covered container. Yield: 40 cheese sticks.

Note: Work with 1 sheet of the pastry at a time, leaving remaining sheet in refrigerator until needed.

Cheddar Pennies

1/2 cup (1 stick) butter or margarine, softened
1 (5-ounce) jar Old English cheese spread
3/4 cup flour
Tabasco sauce to taste
Seasoned salt to taste

Combine the butter and cheese spread in a bowl and mix until blended. Add the flour, Tabasco sauce and seasoned salt, stirring until blended. Shape into 1/2-inch balls. Arrange on a baking sheet. Freeze until firm.

Arrange the frozen cheese balls 2 inches apart on a baking sheet. Bake at 425 degrees in a preheated oven for 8 to 10 minutes or until light brown. Remove to a wire rack to cool. Yield: 50 servings.

Cheesy Spinach Squares

2 (10 ounces each) packages frozen chopped spinach,
    thawed, drained
1/4 cup (1/2 stick) butter
3 eggs
1 cup flour
1 cup milk
1 teaspoon salt
1 teaspoon baking powder
1 pound mozzarella cheese, shredded

Squeeze the excess moisture from the spinach. Place the butter in a 9x13-inch baking pan. Heat at 350 degrees in a preheated oven until melted. Whisk the eggs in a bowl until blended. Add the flour, milk, salt and baking powder, stirring until blended. Stir in the spinach and cheese.

Spoon the spinach mixture into the prepared pan. Bake at 350 degrees for 35 minutes. Cool in pan on a wire rack for 30 minutes or longer. Cut into squares. Serve warm. May be prepared in advance and stored, covered, in the freezer. Reheat at 350 degrees in a preheated oven for 20 minutes. Yield: 25 squares.

Chile Cheese Squares

¼ cup (½ stick) butter
5 eggs
¼ cup flour
½ teaspoon baking powder
¼ teaspoon salt
⅛ to ¼ teaspoon cayenne pepper
2 cups shredded Cheddar cheese
1 cup small curd cottage cheese
1 (4-ounce) can diced green chiles

Place the butter in a 9x9-inch baking pan. Heat at 400 degrees in a preheated oven until melted, tilting the pan to coat the bottom. Whisk the eggs in a bowl until blended. Mix the flour, baking powder, salt and cayenne pepper together. Add to the eggs. Add the Cheddar cheese, cottage cheese and chiles and mix well.

Spoon the cheese mixture into the prepared pan. Bake at 400 degrees for 15 minutes. Reduce the oven temperature to 350 degrees. Bake for 30 to 35 minutes longer or until a knife inserted in the center comes out clean and the top is light brown. Cool in pan on a wire rack for 10 to 15 minutes. Cut into squares. Yield: 36 squares.

Akron once was the western frontier of the United States. In 1785, Portage Path was established as the western boundary by the Treaty of Fort McIntosh between early America and Indian territory. Today's Portage Path roughly follows the original path, first carved by native Americans who "portaged," or traveled, between the Cuyahoga and Tuscarawas rivers.

Chicken Bacon Nuggets

2 large whole boneless skinless chicken breasts, split
1/4 cup orange marmalade
2 tablespoons soy sauce
1/2 teaspoon salt
1/2 teaspoon ginger
1/8 teaspoon garlic powder
1 (8-ounce) package bacon

Cut the chicken into chunks. Combine the orange marmalade, soy sauce, salt, ginger and garlic powder in a bowl and mix well. Add the chicken and stir to coat. Arrange the bacon on a broiler rack in a broiler pan. Broil in a preheated oven for 4 minutes or until partially cooked, turning once. Cut the bacon into halves.

Drain the chicken, reserving the marinade. Wrap each chicken chunk with a bacon half and secure with a wooden pick. Arrange on a broiler rack in a broiler pan. Broil for 5 minutes or until the chicken is cooked through, turning once.

Bring the reserved marinade to a boil in a saucepan, stirring occasionally. Boil for 2 minutes. Brush the bacon with the marinade just before serving. Yield: 15 to 20 servings.

Miniature Drumsticks

3 pounds chicken wings (about 18 wings)
1/2 cup flour
1/2 cup freshly grated Parmesan cheese
1 teaspoon salt
1 teaspoon paprika
1/2 teaspoon oregano
3/4 cup buttermilk
1/4 teaspoon Tabasco sauce
Vegetable oil for frying

Cut the chicken wings at the larger joints, reserving only the larger portion. Combine the flour, cheese, salt, paprika and oregano in a shallow dish and mix well. Combine the buttermilk and Tabasco sauce in a bowl and mix well.

Dip the chicken in the buttermilk mixture and shake to remove excess. Coat with the flour mixture. Heat the oil in a skillet to 365 degrees. Add the chicken. Fry for 5 minutes or until golden brown; drain. Yield: 18 drumsticks.

The first artificial fish bait was developed by Akron's Pflueger Fishing Tackle Company, founded as The Enterprise Manufacturing Company by Ernest F. Pflueger in 1881. Today, the company's classic fishing gear is highly valued by collectors.

Chicken Won Tons with Spicy Mustard Sauce

8 ounces cream cheese, softened
2 cups finely chopped cooked chicken
1 tablespoon finely chopped jalapeño chile
3 tablespoons finely chopped green chiles
2 tablespoons bread crumbs
1 garlic clove, minced
1/2 teaspoon salt
48 won ton wrappers
1 recipe Spicy Mustard Sauce

Combine the cream cheese, chicken, jalapeño chile, green chiles, bread crumbs, garlic and salt in a bowl and mix well. Spoon 1 teaspoon of the cream cheese mixture in the center of each won ton wrapper. Bring the sides of the wrappers to the center and twist or pinch to form a package.

Arrange the won tons on a baking sheet. Bake at 350 degrees in a preheated oven for 10 to 15 minutes or until light brown and crisp. Serve with Spicy Mustard Sauce. Yield: 48 won tons.

Spicy Mustard Sauce
1/2 cup dry mustard
1/2 cup white vinegar
1/2 cup sugar
1 egg yolk, lightly beaten

Combine the dry mustard and vinegar in a glass bowl and mix well. Let stand, covered, at room temperature for 8 to 10 hours. Combine the mustard mixture, sugar and egg yolk in a saucepan and mix well. Cook over low heat until thickened, stirring constantly. May be prepared in advance and stored, covered, in the refrigerator. Yield: 1 cup.

Sweet-and-Sour Chicken Wraps

1 cup chopped cooked chicken
2 tablespoons chopped green onions
1 tablespoon drained canned crushed pineapple
2 tablespoons honey
1 tablespoon soy sauce
2 teaspoons dry mustard
1 (8-count) can crescent rolls
1 egg, beaten
2 teaspoons sesame seeds, toasted

Combine the chicken, green onions and pineapple in a bowl and mix well. Combine the honey, soy sauce and dry mustard in a bowl and mix well. Stir into the chicken mixture.

Unroll the dough. Separate into 4 rectangles, pressing perforations to seal. Cut each rectangle crosswise into halves. Spoon 1 rounded tablespoon of the chicken mixture in the center of each square. Pull the corners to the center and twist to seal. Brush with the egg and sprinkle with the sesame seeds.

Arrange the wraps on an ungreased baking sheet. Bake at 375 degrees in a preheated oven for 10 to 15 minutes or until golden brown. Yield: 8 wraps.

B.F. Goodrich, once headquartered in Akron, helped forge the development of the tire industry. The company was the first to manufacture the clincher tire of 19-ply in 1899, the cord tire for commercial use in 1910, and tubeless automotive tires (which sealed themselves when punctured) in 1947. B.F. Goodrich also manufactured the cord bicycle tire with self-healing treads in 1892.

New England Clam Fritters

1 cup flour
1 teaspoon baking powder
1/8 teaspoon salt
1/2 cup milk
1 egg, lightly beaten
1 (8-ounce) can minced clams
Vegetable shortening for frying

Combine the flour, baking powder and salt in a bowl and mix well. Stir in the milk and egg. Add the clams and mix well.

Add enough shortening to an electric skillet to measure 3 inches when melted. Heat to 300 degrees. Drop the clam mixture by spoonfuls into the hot shortening. Fry until golden brown, turning once. Drain on paper towels. Serve immediately.
Yield: 25 to 30 servings.

Muenster and Ham Bites

1/2 cup (1 stick) margarine, softened
6 tablespoons minced onion
6 tablespoons prepared mustard
2 tablespoons poppy seeds
72 slices party bread
18 slices Muenster cheese, cut into halves
1 1/2 pounds ham, chopped

Combine the margarine, onion, prepared mustard and poppy seeds in a bowl and mix well. Spread the poppy seed mixture on 1 side of half the bread slices. Layer each slice with 1/2 slice of the cheese and some of the ham. Top with the remaining bread slices.

Wrap individually in foil. Arrange in a single layer on a baking sheet. Bake at 350 degrees in a preheated oven for 12 to 15 minutes or until heated through. Yield: 36 servings.

In the first half of the twentieth century, Saalfield Publishing of Akron was the largest publisher of children's books in the world. Among their best known products were Saalfield Muslin Books, printed in bright colors on soft linen, and Shirley Temple books and paper dolls. Their books are collectors items now.

Ham Crescent Snacks

1 (8-count) can crescent rolls
4 thin slices ham
4 teaspoons prepared mustard
1 cup shredded Swiss or Cheddar cheese
1/4 cup sesame seeds

Unroll the dough. Separate into 4 rectangles, pressing perforations to seal. Arrange 1 slice of the ham on each rectangle. Spread with the mustard and sprinkle with the cheese. Roll rectangles up from short end and press edges to seal. Coat with the sesame seeds.

Cut each roll into 5 slices. Arrange the slices cut side down on an ungreased baking sheet. Bake at 375 degrees in a preheated oven for 15 to 20 minutes or until brown. Serve immediately.
Yield: 20 servings.

Deceptively Delicious Dog Delicacies

1 (16-ounce) package frankfurters
1 (16-ounce) package bacon
Brown sugar to taste

Line an 8x8-inch baking pan with foil, allowing an overhang. Cut the frankfurters into quarters. Cut the bacon slices into halves. Wrap each frankfurter quarter with a bacon half and secure with a wooden pick.

Pack the wrapped frankfurters tightly in the prepared pan. Sprinkle generously with brown sugar. Pull the sides of the foil to shift frankfurters closer together and pack tighter.

Bake at 350 degrees in a preheated oven for 1 hour; drain. Serve immediately. Yield: 32 to 40 servings.

Puffed wheat and puffed rice "shot from cannons" are among the cereals once produced in Akron. The puffed rice was actually processed in compressed air hoppers at one of the Quaker Mills. Cascade Plaza in downtown Akron is now located at the site of the mills.

Baby Reubens

Russian or Thousand Island salad dressing
1 loaf party rye bread
1 pound corned beef, thinly sliced
1 (16-ounce) can sauerkraut, drained
8 ounces Swiss cheese, medium sliced, cut into quarters

Spread salad dressing on 1 side of each bread slice. Layer half the bread slices with the corned beef, sauerkraut and cheese. Top with the remaining bread slices dressing side down.

Arrange the sandwiches in a single layer on a baking sheet. Bake at 350 degrees in a preheated oven until the cheese melts. Serve immediately. May secure sandwiches with a wooden pick before serving. Yield: 20 sandwiches.

Sausage Pinwheels

1 pound breakfast sausage
2 (8-count each) cans crescent rolls

Let the sausage stand at room temperature for 15 minutes. Unroll 1 can of the roll dough. Arrange the rectangles to form a large rectangle on a sheet of foil, pressing perforations and edges to seal.

Spread the rectangle with half the sausage. Roll up from short end, pinching edge to seal. Wrap with foil and twist ends of foil to seal. Freeze until just before baking. Repeat the process with the remaining roll dough and sausage.

To serve, let the rolls stand at room temperature for 15 to 20 minutes or until slightly thawed. Cut each roll into 20 slices. Arrange the slices cut side down on a baking sheet. Bake at 350 degrees in a preheated oven for 10 to 15 minutes or until golden brown on both sides. Yield: 40 pinwheels.

Italian Sausage

1 pound Italian sausage links
1 medium onion, sliced, or to taste
1 or 2 green bell peppers, sliced

Pierce the sausage links with a fork. Arrange the sausage in a baking dish. Add just enough water to cover the bottom of the dish. Bake at 350 degrees in a preheated oven for 60 to 70 minutes or until the sausage is cooked through, adding the onion and green peppers 25 minutes before the end of the cooking process. Cut the sausage into bite-size pieces. Serve with the onion and green pepper on miniature rolls if desired.
Yield: 4 to 6 servings.

The Akron area was once the leader nationally in the manufacture of rubber toys. Today, toy rubber dolls from the Sun Rubber Company are prized by collectors.

Tangy Kielbasa Bites

1 (10-ounce) jar currant jelly
1 (8-ounce) jar Dijon mustard
1 link Kielbasa sausage, diagonally sliced

Combine the jelly and Dijon mustard in a saucepan and mix well.
Add the sausage and stir to coat. Cook over medium heat until
heated through, stirring occasionally. Spoon into a fondue pot.
Keep warm over a low flame. Yield: 4 to 6 servings.

Spicy Puff Pastry

1 (17-ounce) package puff pastry
1½ tablespoons Dijon mustard
8 thin slices Genoa salami
1 cup shredded hot pepper cheese

Let the unwrapped puff pastry stand at room temperature for
10 minutes.

Place 1 sheet of the puff pastry on a hard surface. Spread with
the Dijon mustard. Arrange the salami in a single layer over the
pastry. Sprinkle with the cheese. Top with the remaining puff
pastry. Crimp the edges with moistened fingers to seal.

Place the pastry on a nonstick baking sheet. Bake at 400 degrees in
a preheated oven for 15 to 18 minutes or until golden brown. Cut
into bite-size rectangles. Yield: 9 servings.

Pesto Pockets

1/2 cup shredded mozzarella cheese
1/4 cup grated Parmesan cheese
2 (10-count each) cans biscuits
10 teaspoons pesto sauce
1 egg white, beaten
Parmesan cheese to taste
Chopped pine nuts to taste

Combine the mozzarella cheese and 1/4 cup Parmesan cheese in a bowl and mix well. Separate the biscuits. Roll each biscuit on a hard surface into a 4-inch circle. Spread 1/2 teaspoon of the pesto sauce on half of each circle, spreading to within 1/4 inch of the edge. Sprinkle the cheese mixture over the pesto sauce.

Brush the edges of the circles with some of the egg white. Fold over to enclose the filling. Pinch the edges or press the edges with a fork to seal. Brush with the remaining egg white. Sprinkle with the remaining cheese mixture, Parmesan cheese to taste and pine nuts. Bake at 400 degrees in a preheated oven for 8 to 10 minutes or until brown. Yield: 20 servings.

Pesto comes from the Italian word pestare, *meaning "to pound" or "to bruise."*

Tex-Mex Appetizer Tart

1 (1-crust) pie pastry
1½ cups shredded CoJack cheese
½ cup chopped drained roasted red bell pepper
1 (4-ounce) can chopped green chiles
½ cup mayonnaise
¼ cup chopped fresh cilantro or parsley

Place the pastry on an ungreased baking sheet, pressing out the fold lines. Combine the cheese, roasted pepper and chiles in a bowl and mix well. Stir in the mayonnaise. Spread over the pastry to within 1 inch of the edge. Fold the edge over to form a 1-inch border and flute.

Bake at 375 degrees in a preheated oven for 25 to 35 minutes or until golden brown. Sprinkle with the cilantro. Cut into wedges. Serve warm. Yield: 16 servings.

Hot Tuna Melts

1 (7-ounce) can water-pack tuna, drained
1/2 cup shredded Cheddar cheese
1/3 cup pickle relish
1/4 cup chopped onion
Mayonnaise-type salad dressing
32 to 40 slices party bread

Combine the tuna, cheese, pickle relish and onion in a bowl and mix well. Spread a thin layer of salad dressing on 1 side of each bread slice. Spread with 1 tablespoon of the tuna mixture and smooth to the edge.

Arrange the slices filling side up on a baking sheet. Broil in a preheated oven for 5 to 7 minutes or until the cheese melts. Place 2 slices together to form a sandwich. Yield: 16 to 20 servings.

_____

"The greatest dishes are very simple dishes."

—*Escoffier*

_____

openings

classic

In This Section

Hot Buttered Rum

1/2 gallon cider
1 quart dark rum
1/4 cup packed brown sugar
1/4 cup (1/2 stick) butter
1/8 teaspoon cinnamon

Heat the cider in a large saucepan until simmering. Stir in the rum, brown sugar, butter and cinnamon. Heat until the brown sugar dissolves and the butter melts, stirring occasionally. Ladle into mugs. Yield: 15 servings.

Party Punch

1 liter Hawaiian punch
1 liter ginger ale
1/2 liter club soda
1 (6-ounce) can frozen lemonade concentrate
2 teaspoons sugar
Ice ring
Sherbet

Combine the Hawaiian punch, ginger ale, club soda, lemonade concentrate and sugar in a punch bowl and mix well. Add the ice ring. Add 2 to 4 small scoops of your favorite sherbet to the punch bowl. Ladle into punch cups. Recipe may be halved. Yield: 25 to 30 servings.

Before making it big in Hollywood, Ohio native Clark Gable worked in Akron.

Artichoke Dip

2 (14 ounces each) cans artichoke hearts, drained
1 1/2 cups grated Parmesan cheese
1 1/2 cups mayonnaise
1/4 cup dry white wine
4 garlic cloves, minced
Paprika to taste
Parsley flakes to taste
Tortilla chips
Assorted party crackers

Mash the artichokes in a bowl. Stir in the cheese, mayonnaise, wine and garlic. Spoon into a baking dish. Sprinkle with paprika and parsley flakes.

Bake at 450 degrees in a preheated oven for 25 minutes or until brown and bubbly. Serve immediately with tortilla chips and/or assorted party crackers. Yield: 20 to 25 servings.

Cheddar Artichoke Dip

1 (14-ounce) can artichoke hearts, drained, chopped
1 1/4 cups shredded sharp Cheddar cheese
1 cup grated Parmesan cheese
1/2 cup chopped green onions
1 garlic clove, minced
1/2 cup mayonnaise
Assorted party crackers

Combine the artichokes, Cheddar cheese, Parmesan cheese, green onions and garlic in a bowl and mix well. Stir in the mayonnaise. Spoon into a baking dish. Bake at 350 degrees in a preheated oven for 20 minutes or until bubbly. Serve immediately with assorted party crackers. Yield: 8 servings.

Hot Artichoke Dip

1 tablespoon sesame seeds
2 (8 ounces each) cans artichoke hearts, drained, rinsed
Juice of 1/2 lemon
1 cup freshly grated Parmesan cheese
1 cup mayonnaise
Assorted party crackers
Assorted party breads

Heat the sesame seeds in a small sauté pan over medium heat just until the sesame seeds begin to turn golden brown, stirring constantly. Process the artichokes in a food processor fitted with a metal blade until finely chopped or chop by hand.

Drizzle the lemon juice over the artichokes in a bowl. Stir in the cheese and mayonnaise. Spoon into a 1- or 2-quart baking dish. Sprinkle with the sesame seeds. Bake at 350 degrees in a preheated oven for 20 to 25 minutes or until bubbly. Serve with assorted party crackers and party breads. May substitute reduced-fat mayonnaise for the mayonnaise. Yield: 20 servings.

"It is good for a man to eat thistles, and to remember that he is an ass. But an artichoke is the best of thistles, and the man who enjoys {them} has the satisfaction of feeling that he is an ass of good taste."

—Kettner's Book of
the Table, 1877
E.S. Dallas (1828-1879)

Savory Artichoke and Spinach Dip

1 (10-ounce) package frozen chopped spinach, thawed, drained
1 1/4 cups coarsely grated Parmesan cheese
1 cup mayonnaise
1 garlic clove, crushed
8 to 10 artichoke hearts, coarsely chopped
Chopped green onions (optional)
Butter crackers

Squeeze the excess moisture from the spinach. Combine the cheese, mayonnaise, garlic, artichokes and spinach in the order listed in a bowl, mixing well after each addition. Spoon into an ungreased quiche dish or baking dish and press lightly. Bake at 325 degrees in a preheated oven for 25 to 30 minutes or until brown and bubbly. Sprinkle with chopped green onions. Serve warm with butter crackers. Yield: 8 to 12 servings.

Spicy Artichoke Dip

1 (16-ounce) can marinated or water-pack artichoke hearts,
    drained, chopped
1 pound mozzarella cheese, shredded
1/4 cup grated Parmesan cheese
1/4 cup chopped green chiles
1 teaspoon garlic salt
Pepper to taste
1/2 cup mayonnaise
1/2 cup sour cream
Garlic bagel chips
Tortilla chips

Combine the artichokes, mozzarella cheese, Parmesan cheese, chiles, garlic salt and pepper in a bowl and mix well. Stir in the mayonnaise and sour cream. Spoon into a baking dish. Bake at 350 degrees in a preheated oven for 30 to 35 minutes or until brown and bubbly. Serve hot with garlic bagel chips and/or tortilla chips. Yield: 15 servings.

Baked Crab Dip

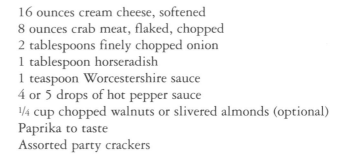

16 ounces cream cheese, softened
8 ounces crab meat, flaked, chopped
2 tablespoons finely chopped onion
1 tablespoon horseradish
1 teaspoon Worcestershire sauce
4 or 5 drops of hot pepper sauce
¼ cup chopped walnuts or slivered almonds (optional)
Paprika to taste
Assorted party crackers

Beat the cream cheese in a mixing bowl for 1 to 2 minutes or until creamy and smooth, scraping the bowl occasionally. Add the crab meat, onion, horseradish, Worcestershire sauce and hot pepper sauce and mix well. Spread the crab mixture evenly in a 9-inch round baking dish. Top with the walnuts. Sprinkle with paprika. Bake, uncovered, at 375 degrees in a preheated oven for 20 minutes or until golden brown. Serve warm with assorted party crackers. Yield: 3 cups.

Hot Crab Dip

24 ounces cream cheese
1½ cups Alaskan crab meat
½ cup mayonnaise
¼ cup chopped onion
¼ cup white wine
1 teaspoon prepared horseradish
2 teaspoons Dijon mustard
2 teaspoons confectioners' sugar
Salt and pepper to taste
Paprika to taste
Assorted party crackers

Combine the cream cheese, crab meat, mayonnaise, onion, white wine, horseradish, Dijon mustard, confectioners' sugar, salt and pepper in a saucepan. Bring to a boil, stirring constantly. Spoon into a ceramic fondue pot. Sprinkle with paprika. Serve warm with assorted party crackers. Yield: 20 servings.

In 1923, Firestone Tire and Rubber Company, once headquartered in Akron, was the first to manufacture balloon tires on a regular basis. The company also developed and manufactured the modern nonskid tire, developed by Firestone's Stacy G. Carkuff back in 1908 and patented in 1914. The angle formation on the edges of the raised portions molded on the tire helped prevent skidding in all directions.

Sherry Crab Dip

24 ounces cream cheese
1/2 cup mayonnaise
1/3 to 2/3 cup sherry
2 teaspoons prepared mustard
2 teaspoons confectioners' sugar
1/8 teaspoon garlic salt
1 pound imitation crab meat, chopped
Melba toast rounds
Assorted party crackers

Heat the cream cheese in a double boiler over simmering water until softened, stirring frequently. Add the mayonnaise, sherry, prepared mustard, confectioners' sugar and garlic salt, stirring until blended. Fold in the crab meat. Cook just until heated through, stirring frequently. Spoon the crab dip into a chafing dish or into an ovenproof dish and place on a warming tray. Serve with melba toast rounds and/or assorted party crackers. Yield: 3 cups.

Hummus bi Tahini

3 (15 ounces each) cans garbanzo beans or chick-peas, drained
1/2 cup puréed mild banana pepper rings, drained
1/2 cup plus 2 tablespoons fresh lemon juice
1/3 cup tahini (sesame seed paste)
3 tablespoons olive oil
1/2 teaspoon Hungarian paprika
1 garlic clove
Salt to taste
Chopped fresh parsley
Assorted party breads
Assorted party crackers

Combine the garbanzo beans, puréed banana pepper, lemon juice, tahini, olive oil, paprika, garlic and salt in a blender or food processor container. Process until of the consistency of a smooth thick paste. Spoon into a serving bowl. Sprinkle with chopped fresh parsley and additional Hungarian paprika. Drizzle with additional olive oil if desired. Serve with party bread and/or assorted party crackers. Yield: 15 to 20 servings.

Seven-Layer Dip

1 (9-ounce) can bean dip
1 large ripe avocado, chopped
2 tablespoons lemon juice
$1/2$ teaspoon garlic salt
$1/2$ cup sour cream
1 envelope taco seasoning mix
2 large tomatoes, chopped
$1/2$ cup sliced black olives
1 (9-ounce) can jalapeño and Cheddar cheese dip
$1/2$ cup chopped green onions
Tortilla chips

Spread the bean dip in a shallow 2-quart dish. Sprinkle with the avocado. Drizzle with the lemon juice and sprinkle with the garlic salt. Combine the sour cream and seasoning mix in a bowl and mix well. Spread over the prepared layers. Layer with the tomatoes and black olives. Spread with the jalapeño and Cheddar cheese dip and sprinkle with the green onions. Serve with tortilla chips. Yield: 6 cups.

Personalities who trace their beginnings to the Akron area:

ABC's 20/20 anchor Hugh Downs
Star Trek Next Generation's star Gates McFadden
NBC's Providence star Melina Kanakaredes
Supermodel and actress Angie Everhart
The late Grandpa Jones of Hee-Haw fame
Musician James Ingram
Character actor and longtime "Maytag repairman" Jesse White
"Third Rock from the Sun" actor John Lithgow, who once lived here with his family

Summit Sunburst

1 (30-ounce) can refried beans
1 (4-ounce) can chopped mild green chiles
1 cup mayonnaise
1 cup sour cream
1 recipe Chunky Guacamole (below)
1 (14-ounce) can black olives, drained, coarsely chopped
1 (10-ounce) jar green olives, drained, coarsely chopped
1½ pounds sharp Cheddar cheese, shredded
Sour cream to taste
Tortilla chips

Combine the refried beans and chiles in a bowl and mix well. Combine the mayonnaise and 1 cup sour cream in a bowl and mix well.

Spread the bean mixture on a round high-lipped platter. Spread with the Chunky Guacamole and then with the mayonnaise mixture. Sprinkle with the black olives and green olives. Top with the cheese. Top with dollops of sour cream to taste. Arrange tortilla chips around the platter to resemble a sunburst. Serve with a basket of tortilla chips. Yield: 20 servings.

Chunky Guacamole

2 large ripe avocados
1 large ripe tomato, chopped
½ red onion, coarsely chopped
1 tablespoon lemon juice
1 teaspoon salt (optional)
¼ teaspoon white pepper
Tortilla chips

Mash the avocados in a bowl until of a chunky consistency. Stir in the tomato, onion, lemon juice, salt and white pepper. Serve with tortilla chips. Yield: 8 to 10 servings.

Spinach Dip

1 (10-ounce) package frozen chopped spinach, thawed, drained
1 cup sour cream
1 cup mayonnaise
1/2 medium onion, chopped
1 (8-ounce) can water chestnuts, drained, chopped
1 envelope vegetable soup mix
1 (1-pound) round loaf pumpernickel or German rye bread

Squeeze the excess moisture from the spinach. Combine the spinach, sour cream, mayonnaise, onion, water chestnuts and soup mix in a bowl and mix well.

Hollow out the bread loaf carefully, leaving a 1/2-inch shell. Tear the bread from the center into bite-size pieces. Spoon the dip into the bread shell. Arrange on a platter. Surround with the bread. The dip may be prepared in advance and stored, covered, in the refrigerator until serving time. Yield: 15 servings.

Hot Spinach Dip

1 (10-ounce) package frozen chopped spinach, thawed, drained
1/4 cup (1/2 stick) butter
1/4 cup flour
1/2 teaspoon salt
1/4 teaspoon pepper
2 cups milk
8 ounces hot pepper cheese, cubed
Corn or tortilla chips

Squeeze the excess mixture from the spinach. Heat the butter in a saucepan until melted. Stir in the flour, salt and pepper. Cook over low heat until thickened, stirring constantly. Remove from heat.

Stir in the milk. Bring to a boil, stirring constantly. Boil for 1 minute, stirring constantly. Remove from heat. Add the spinach and cheese, stirring until the cheese melts. Serve warm with corn chips or tortilla chips. Yield: 8 servings.

Commonly served as an appetizer in the United States, bruschetta originated in Italy as a workman's midday snack.

Mexican Spinach Dip

1 (10-ounce) package frozen chopped spinach, thawed, drained
8 ounces cream cheese, softened
1/3 cup half-and-half
2 cups shredded Monterey Jack cheese
2 tomatoes, chopped
1/2 cup chopped green onions
1 (4-ounce) can chopped green chiles, drained
1 tablespoon chopped fresh cilantro
1/4 teaspoon Tabasco sauce
Tortilla chips

Squeeze the excess moisture from the spinach. Beat the cream cheese and half-and-half in a mixing bowl until blended. Stir in the spinach, cheese, tomatoes, green onions, chiles, cilantro and Tabasco sauce. Spoon into a 1-quart baking dish sprayed with nonstick cooking spray or coated with butter. Bake at 400 degrees in a preheated oven for 20 to 25 minutes or until bubbly. Serve warm with tortilla chips. Yield: 10 servings.

Taco Dip

2 cups sour cream
8 ounces cream cheese, softened
1 envelope mild or hot taco seasoning mix
Shredded lettuce
1 tomato, chopped
4 ounces Cheddar cheese, shredded
Sliced black olives
Tortilla chips

Beat the sour cream and cream cheese in a mixing bowl until blended. Stir in the seasoning mix. Spread in a 9x13-inch dish. Top with shredded lettuce, tomato and cheese in the order listed. Sprinkle with black olives. Chill, covered, for 2 hours before serving. Serve with tortilla chips. Yield: 15 to 20 servings.

Fresh Fruit Pizza

3/4 cup (1 1/2 sticks) butter, softened
2/3 cup sugar
2 cups flour
1/4 cup milk
8 ounces cream cheese, softened
1/4 cup sugar
2 tablespoons sour cream
1/2 teaspoon grated lemon zest
1/2 teaspoon vanilla extract
Sliced fresh strawberries, peaches, kiwifruit, blueberries, grapes,
    raspberries, pineapple and/or bananas
3/4 cup orange juice
1/4 cup sugar
1 tablespoon cornstarch

Combine the butter and 2/3 cup sugar in a bowl and mix well. Stir
in the flour and milk. Press over the bottom and up the side of a
12-inch pizza pan. Bake at 400 degrees in a preheated oven for
14 to 16 minutes or until light brown. Let stand until cool.

Combine the cream cheese, 1/4 cup sugar, sour cream, lemon zest
and vanilla in a bowl and mix well. Spread evenly over the baked
layer. Arrange the desired fruit over the cream cheese mixture.

Combine the orange juice, 1/4 cup sugar and cornstarch in a
saucepan. Bring to a low boil. Boil for 1 to 2 minutes or until of
a glaze consistency, stirring occasionally. Cool for 10 minutes.
Drizzle over the prepared layers. Chill, covered, until serving
time. Yield: 10 to 12 servings.

*The John Brown House
was the Akron home of
abolitionist John Brown
in the 1840s when he
was a partner in the wool
business with Simon
Perkins, Jr., the son of
Akron's founder. The house
later became the meeting
place for the Portage Golf
Club, which evolved into
Portage Country Club,
another Akron landmark.*

Garden Salad Pizza

2 (8-count each) cans crescent rolls
16 ounces cream cheese, softened
3/4 cup mayonnaise
1 envelope ranch salad dressing mix
1 green bell pepper, chopped
1 tomato, chopped
1/2 (16-ounce) can black olives, drained, sliced
1/2 cup chopped mushrooms
1/2 cup chopped broccoli
1/2 cup chopped cauliflower
1/2 cup shredded Cheddar cheese
1/4 cup grated Romano or Parmesan cheese

Unroll the dough. Separate into rectangles. Pat the dough
over the bottom and up the sides of a 10x15-inch baking sheet,
pressing the edges and perforations to seal. Bake at 350 degrees in
a preheated oven using package directions. Let stand until cool.

Beat the cream cheese, mayonnaise and dressing mix in a bowl
until blended, scraping the bowl occasionally. Spread over the
baked layer. Top with the green pepper, tomato, black olives,
mushrooms, broccoli and cauliflower. Sprinkle with the Cheddar
cheese and Romano cheese. Serve immediately or chill, covered,
until serving time. Yield: 10 to 12 servings.

Pepperoni Bread

1 loaf French bread
2 cups mayonnaise
1 cup grated Parmesan cheese
1½ cups shredded Cheddar cheese
⅛ teaspoon garlic powder
8 ounces pepperoni, sliced

Slice the loaf lengthwise into halves. Combine the mayonnaise, Parmesan cheese, Cheddar cheese and garlic powder in a bowl and mix well. Spread the cut side of each half of the bread with the cheese mixture. Top with the pepperoni slices. Arrange the bread halves on a baking sheet.

Bake at 350 degrees in a preheated oven for 15 to 20 minutes or until golden brown and bubbly. Cut into slices. Serve immediately. Yield: 15 to 20 servings.

Built in 1929, the Goodyear Airdock (now owned by Loral) was one of the hot tourist attractions of the early 1930s. It was built to house huge airships nearly 800 feet long (about four times the length of the current Goodyear blimps). In its day, this airship hangar was the world's largest building without interior supports. In fact, it is so huge that it has its own weather conditions inside. It covers eight acres and is the height of a 22-story building. It boasts 55,000,000 cubic feet of interior space and could cover eight football fields in overall floor space.

Cheese Ball

8 ounces cream cheese, softened
8 ounces Cheddar cheese, shredded, softened
1 teaspoon Worcestershire sauce
1 small onion, chopped
3 cups chopped walnuts

Combine the cream cheese and Cheddar cheese in a bowl and mix well. Add the Worcestershire sauce and mix until blended. Stir in the onion. Chill, covered, for 8 to 10 hours. Shape the cheese mixture into a ball. Coat with the walnuts. Serve with assorted party crackers. Yield: 16 servings.

Bleu Cheese Ball

16 ounces cream cheese, softened
1 (5-ounce) jar Old English sharp Cheddar cheese spread
5 ounces bleu cheese, crumbled
1/4 cup chopped onion
1 tablespoon Worcestershire sauce
1 tablespoon chopped fresh parsley
1/8 teaspoon salt
Chopped walnuts
Assorted party crackers

Combine the cream cheese, cheese spread, bleu cheese, onion, Worcestershire sauce, parsley and salt in a mixer bowl or blender. Beat or process until blended, scraping the bowl occasionally. Chill, covered, for 8 hours. Shape the cheese mixture into a ball. Coat with walnuts. Chill, wrapped in plastic wrap, for 8 hours longer. Serve with assorted party crackers. Yield: 25 servings.

Hearty Cheese Ball

16 ounces cream cheese, softened
1 (6-ounce) package dried beef, finely chopped
2 green onions, finely chopped
1 teaspoon Worcestershire sauce or soy sauce
Chopped fresh parsley
Assorted party crackers

Combine the cream cheese, dried beef, green onions and
Worcestershire sauce in a bowl and mix well. Shape into a ball.
Chill, wrapped in plastic wrap, for 8 to 10 hours. Coat with
parsley. Serve with assorted party crackers.
Yield: 15 to 20 servings.

Crab Meat Cheese Ball

16 ounces cream cheese, softened
2 (6 ounces each) cans crab meat, drained
1 (12-ounce) jar cocktail sauce
Leaf lettuce and endive
Assorted party crackers

Beat the cream cheese in a mixer bowl until creamy. Add the
crab meat and mix well. Shape into a ball. Chill, covered, for 2 to
3 hours. Arrange the cheese ball on a serving platter lined with
leaf lettuce and endive. Pour the cocktail sauce over the top. Serve
with assorted party crackers. Yield: 20 to 25 servings.

The Civic Theatre in Akron, one of the first combination vaudeville stage and movie theaters, was completed in 1929. John Eberson, the architect, is known as the Frank Lloyd Wright of theater design. Its sparkling night sky and thunderous pipe organ still delight crowds today.

Hot Crab Spread

1½ pounds crab meat
24 ounces cream cheese, softened
1 pound medium Cheddar or Swiss cheese, shredded
2 cups coffee cream
2 cups sour cream
¼ cup prepared mustard
1 small onion, minced
⅛ to ¼ teaspoon Worcestershire sauce
Assorted party crackers

Combine the crab meat, cream cheese, Cheddar cheese, coffee cream, sour cream, prepared mustard, onion and Worcestershire sauce in a bowl and mix well. Spoon into a baking dish. Bake at 325 degrees in a preheated oven for 20 minutes. Serve warm with assorted party crackers. Yield: 40 to 50 servings.

Hot Crab Meat Spread

2 cups shredded crab meat
2 cups shredded Swiss cheese
2 tablespoons chopped green onions
1 cup mayonnaise
2 teaspoons lemon juice
Paprika to taste
Assorted party crackers

Combine the crab meat, cheese and green onions in a bowl. Stir in the mayonnaise and lemon juice. Spoon into a 10-inch deep round baking dish. Sprinkle with paprika. Bake at 325 degrees in a preheated oven for 15 to 20 minutes or until bubbly. Serve with assorted party crackers. May substitute imitation crab meat for the crab meat. Yield: 12 to 15 servings.

"Plains Special" Cheese Ring

1 pound sharp Cheddar cheese, shredded
1 cup finely chopped nuts
1 small onion, grated
1 cup mayonnaise
1/8 teaspoon cayenne pepper
Black pepper to taste
Strawberry preserves
Assorted party crackers

Combine the cheese, nuts and onion in a bowl and mix well. Stir in the mayonnaise, cayenne pepper and black pepper. Pack the cheese mixture into a 5-cup ring mold or any fancy 4-cup mold. Chill, covered, for 8 to 10 hours.

Invert the cheese ring onto a serving platter. Fill the center with strawberry preserves and surround with assorted party crackers. Serve strawberry preserves on the side if not using a ring mold. Yield: 20 servings.

Akronite Mina Miller, daughter of Chautauqua, New York co-founder Lewis Miller, married inventor Thomas Edison in Akron.

Barbecued Chicken Wings

3 pounds chicken wings (about 16 wings)
Salt and pepper to taste
1 1/2 cups barbecue sauce
1/2 cup honey
1 1/2 teaspoons prepared or spicy mustard
2 teaspoons Worcestershire sauce
2 teaspoons hot pepper sauce, or to taste

Separate the chicken wings at the joints, discarding the tips.
Sprinkle with salt and pepper. Arrange the chicken in a single
layer on a broiler rack in a broiler pan. Broil 4 inches from the
heat source in a preheated oven for 10 minutes; turn. Broil for
10 minutes longer. Place the chicken in a 2-quart slow cooker.

Combine the barbecue sauce, honey, mustard, Worcestershire
sauce and hot pepper sauce in a bowl and mix well. Pour over the
chicken. Cook, covered, on Low for 4 to 5 hours or on High for
2 1/2 hours, stirring several times. Yield: 32 servings.

Chicken Wings in Honey Sauce

3 pounds chicken wings (about 16 wings)
Salt and pepper to taste
2 cups honey
1 cup soy sauce
1/2 cup catsup
1/4 cup vegetable oil
3 garlic cloves, minced

Separate the chicken wings at the joints, discarding the tips.
Sprinkle with salt and pepper. Arrange the chicken in a single
layer on a broiler rack in a broiler pan. Broil 4 inches from the
heat source in a preheated oven for 10 minutes; turn. Broil for
10 minutes longer.

Place the chicken in a 2-quart slow cooker. Combine the honey,
soy sauce, catsup, oil and garlic in a bowl and mix well. Pour over
the chicken. Cook, covered, on Low for 5 to 6 hours or on High for
2 1/2 hours, stirring several times. Yield: 32 servings.

Teriyaki Chicken Wings

3 pounds chicken wings (about 16 wings)
1 cup soy sauce
1 cup packed brown sugar
1 onion, chopped
1/4 cup dry sherry
1 1/2 teaspoons ground ginger
3 garlic cloves, minced

Separate the chicken wings at the joints, discarding the tips.
Arrange the chicken in a single layer on a broiler rack in a broiler
pan. Broil 4 inches from the heat source in a preheated oven for
10 minutes; turn. Broil for 10 minutes longer.

Place the chicken in a 2-quart slow cooker. Combine the soy
sauce, brown sugar, onion, sherry, ginger and garlic in a large
bowl and mix well. Pour evenly over the chicken. Cook, covered,
on Low for 5 to 6 hours or on High for 2 1/2 to 3 hours, stirring
several times. Yield: 32 servings.

*Akron has been recognized
as one of the cloudiest cities
in America.*

Cocktail Meatballs

1 pound ground beef
2 tablespoons bread crumbs
1 egg, lightly beaten
1/2 teaspoon salt
2 tablespoons margarine
1/3 cup finely chopped green bell pepper
1/3 cup chopped onion
1 (10-ounce) can tomato soup
2 tablespoons brown sugar
4 teaspoons Worcestershire sauce
1 tablespoon prepared mustard
1 tablespoon vinegar

Combine the ground beef, bread crumbs, egg and salt in a bowl
and mix well. Shape into 50 meatballs. Arrange in a 9x13-inch
baking pan. Broil until brown, turning once; drain.

Heat the margarine in a saucepan until melted. Add the green
pepper and onion and mix well. Cook until tender, stirring
constantly. Stir in the soup, brown sugar, Worcestershire sauce,
prepared mustard and vinegar. Pour over the meatballs. Bake,
covered, at 350 degrees in a preheated oven for 20 minutes.
Yield: 50 meatballs.

Piquant Meatballs

1 pound ground beef
1 pound ground sausage
1/2 cup cracker crumbs
1/4 cup grated Parmesan cheese
2 eggs, beaten
1 (14-ounce) bottle catsup
1 (10-ounce) jar grape jelly
1/2 cup packed brown sugar
1/2 envelope French salad dressing mix
1/2 teaspoon garlic powder

Combine the ground beef, sausage, cracker crumbs, cheese and eggs in a bowl and mix well. Shape into 1-inch balls. Arrange the meatballs in a shallow baking pan. Bake at 375 degrees in a preheated oven for 20 minutes, turning occasionally; drain.

Combine the catsup, jelly, brown sugar, dressing mix and garlic powder in a saucepan and mix well. Add the meatballs and mix gently. Simmer for 20 minutes or until the meatballs are cooked through and hot, stirring occasionally. Yield: 84 meatballs.

"Wonder is the beginning of Wisdom."

—*Greek proverb*

Stuffed Mushrooms

12 ounces fresh mushrooms (about 12 mushrooms)
1 tablespoon olive oil
¼ cup chopped onion
1 garlic clove, crushed
⅓ cup bread crumbs
3 tablespoons grated Parmesan cheese
1 tablespoon chopped fresh parsley
⅛ teaspoon oregano

Remove the mushroom stems and finely chop the stems. Arrange the mushroom caps in a single layer in a greased 9x13-inch baking dish. Heat the olive oil in a skillet. Add the chopped mushroom stems, onion and garlic and mix well. Sauté until the onion is tender.

Combine the bread crumbs, cheese, parsley and oregano in a bowl and mix well. Stir in the sautéed mixture. Spoon into the mushroom caps. Bake at 375 degrees in a preheated oven for 15 to 20 minutes or until brown and heated through. Yield: 12 servings.

Bacon-Stuffed Mushrooms

2 cartons fresh mushrooms
1/4 cup (1/2 stick) to 1/2 cup (1 stick) butter, melted
10 slices crisp-fried bacon, crumbled
1 1/2 cups shredded Cheddar cheese
1 small onion, chopped
3/4 cup mayonnaise
Garlic salt to taste

Clean the mushrooms; remove and discard the stems. Set aside. Pour the butter over the bottom of a 9x13-inch baking dish, tilting the pan to cover the bottom. Combine the bacon, cheese and onion in a bowl and mix well. Stir in the mayonnaise and garlic salt.

Fill the mushroom caps with the bacon mixture. Arrange the mushrooms in a single layer in the prepared dish. Bake, covered with foil, at 325 degrees in a preheated oven for 15 minutes or until heated through. Yield: 20 to 24 servings.

At the turn of the twentieth century, Akron was home to a large number of breweries, perhaps to quench the thirst of its population, which at that time was predominantly of German descent.

Spinach-Stuffed Mushrooms

1/2 (10-ounce) package fresh spinach, finely chopped
    (about 3 packed cups)
4 ounces reduced-fat Cheddar cheese, shredded
1/4 cup chopped walnuts
2 tablespoons plain bread crumbs
2 tablespoons Dijon mustard
2 tablespoons nonfat mayonnaise
1 teaspoon pepper
12 medium mushroom caps

Combine the spinach, cheese, walnuts and bread crumbs in a bowl
and mix well. Stir in a mixture of the Dijon mustard, mayonnaise
and pepper. Fill the mushroom caps with the spinach mixture.

Arrange the mushrooms in a single layer in a baking pan. Add
just enough water to the pan to measure 1/4 inch. Tent the pan
with foil. Bake at 400 degrees in a preheated oven for 30 minutes;
remove the foil. Bake for 10 minutes longer or until the
mushrooms are tender and heated through. Yield: 12 servings.

Low-Fat Blooming Onion

1 (1-pound) Spanish or Vidalia onion or any super-sweet onion
1 teaspoon vegetable oil
1/4 ounce cornflake crumbs
1/8 teaspoon red pepper flakes
1/8 teaspoon seasoned salt
1 egg white
Horseradish Dip (page 107)

Trim the root end of the onion so it will stand upright. Slice
1/2 inch from the top of the onion; discard the papery skin. Cut
triangular slices to the center of the onion, slicing from the top to
within 1/2 inch of the bottom and working your way around the
onion to make several petals. Place the onion in a microwave-safe
dish. Drizzle with the oil. Microwave, covered, on High for 11/2 to
2 minutes or until the onion is slightly tender and the petals
begin to separate.

Combine the cornflake crumbs, red pepper and seasoned salt in a
bowl and mix well. Beat the egg white in a bowl until foamy.
Dip the onion into the egg white, coating the petals completely.
Place in a 2-cup round baking dish sprayed with nonstick cooking
spray. Sprinkle with the cornflake mixture. Bake at 350 degrees in
a preheated oven for 10 to 12 minutes or until brown and crisp.
Serve immediately with the Horseradish Dip.
Yield: 4 to 6 servings.

The world's largest model train display is located in Akron.

Horseradish Dip

½ cup nonfat sour cream
2 teaspoons reduced-fat mayonnaise
2 teaspoons prepared horseradish
½ small garlic clove, finely minced

Combine the sour cream, mayonnaise, horseradish and garlic in a bowl and mix well. May be prepared up to 2 days in advance and stored, covered, in the refrigerator. Yield: 4 to 6 servings.

Pizza Roll

1 loaf frozen bread dough
½ cup canned pizza sauce
½ cup chopped green bell pepper
½ cup sliced mushrooms
2 to 3 ounces pepperoni, sliced
½ cup shredded mozzarella cheese
1 egg white, lightly beaten

Thaw the bread dough using package directions. Let rise using package directions. Pat the dough into a rectangle on a greased baking sheet. Spread the pizza sauce lengthwise down the center in a 3-inch-wide strip. Arrange the green pepper, mushrooms and pepperoni over the pizza sauce. Sprinkle with the cheese.

Fold the long sides of the rectangle over to enclose the filling. Brush lightly with the egg white. Bake at 350 degrees in a preheated oven for 15 to 20 minutes or until light brown. Cool slightly. Cut into slices and serve warm. Yield: 6 to 8 servings.

Bacon and Cheese Potato Skins

4 medium unpeeled baking potatoes
3/4 cup shredded reduced-fat Cheddar cheese
4 slices crisp-fried turkey bacon, crumbled
1 tablespoon minced fresh chives
1/4 cup nonfat sour cream

Arrange the potatoes on a baking sheet sprayed with nonstick cooking spray. Bake at 425 degrees in a preheated oven for 1 hour or until tender. Cool slightly. Cut each potato lengthwise into halves. Scoop out the pulp, leaving a 1/4-inch shell. Reserve the pulp for another use.

Arrange the potato shells on a baking sheet. Spray the cavities of the shells with nonstick cooking spray.

Bake at 425 degrees in a preheated oven for 8 minutes or until crisp. Sprinkle with the cheese. Bake for 5 minutes longer or until the cheese melts. Sprinkle with the bacon and chives. Serve with the sour cream. Yield: 8 servings.

Akron is known as the "Birthplace of the Trucking Industry" and is home and headquarters for some of the nation's largest commercial carriers.

Tiropitas

8 ounces feta cheese
8 ounces ricotta cheese
1/3 cup chopped fresh parsley
1 egg
1/8 teaspoon salt
1/8 teaspoon nutmeg
1 (1-pound) package phyllo pastry, thawed
3/4 cup (1 1/2 sticks) unsalted butter, melted

Combine the feta cheese, ricotta cheese, parsley, egg, salt and nutmeg in a food processor container. Process until blended.

Unroll the phyllo and cover with waxed paper topped with a damp towel to prevent it from drying out, removing 1 sheet at a time. Cut each sheet into six or seven 2- to 3-inch strips. Cover the strips until needed.

Brush 1 strip with some of the butter. Top with a second strip and brush with some of the butter. Spoon approximately 1 1/2 teaspoons of the cheese mixture on the corner of the strip. Fold the corner over to the opposite edge to cover the filling, forming a triangle. Continue folding as for a flag. Place the triangle on a parchment-lined baking sheet. Cover to prevent drying out. Repeat the process with the remaining pastry strips, butter and cheese mixture.

Arrange the triangles 1 inch apart on a baking sheet. Bake at 350 degrees in a preheated oven for 10 to 15 minutes or until puffed and light brown. Cool slightly before serving. For variety, add 10 ounces drained cooked frozen spinach. Yield: 60 to 70 servings.

Sauerkraut Balls

1 pound bulk sausage
4 ounces ground beef
1/2 cup chopped onion
3 tablespoons snipped fresh parsley
1 teaspoon each garlic powder, salt and sugar
1/2 teaspoon dry mustard
1/8 teaspoon pepper
1 to 2 pounds drained sauerkraut, chopped
1/2 cup bread crumbs
1 egg, beaten
1/4 cup milk
2 eggs, beaten
Seasoned bread crumbs
Hot Sweet Mustard Sauce (page 111)

Brown the sausage and ground beef with the onion, parsley, garlic powder, salt, sugar, dry mustard and pepper in a skillet, stirring until the sausage and ground beef are crumbly; drain. Stir in the sauerkraut. Add 1/2 cup bread crumbs and 1 egg and mix well. Chill, covered, in the refrigerator. Shape the sausage mixture into 1-inch balls. Dip the balls in a mixture of the milk and 2 eggs. Coat with seasoned bread crumbs. Arrange the balls on a broiler rack in a broiler pan. Broil in a preheated oven until golden brown; drain. Serve with Hot Sweet Mustard Sauce. May freeze the sauerkraut balls before broiling for future use. Yield: variable.

Sauerkraut balls are the official food of Akron.

Hot Sweet Mustard Sauce

¼ cup dry mustard
⅔ cup water
¼ cup sugar
1½ tablespoons cornstarch
½ teaspoon salt
⅓ cup white vinegar

Combine the dry mustard with just enough of the water in a bowl until the mixture is of a pasty consistency. Let stand for several minutes. Combine the sugar, cornstarch and salt in a saucepan and mix well. Stir in the remaining water. Add the vinegar; mix well. Cook over low heat for 5 minutes, stirring constantly. Remove from heat. Let stand until cool. Stir in the mustard mixture. Yield: 1 cup.

Sauerkraut Balls with Ham

1 onion, chopped
¼ cup (½ stick) margarine
1⅓ cups ground ham
½ garlic clove, minced
¼ cup flour
2½ cups coarsely chopped drained sauerkraut
½ cup beef broth
1½ cups milk
1 egg
Bread crumbs, cornflake crumbs, flour
Vegetable oil for frying

Sauté the onion in the margarine in a skillet until light brown. Stir in the ham and garlic. Sauté until the ham is light brown. Add ¼ cup flour and mix well. Cook until heated through, stirring frequently. Stir in the sauerkraut and broth. Cook until the mixture is the consistency of a stiff paste, stirring frequently. Let stand until cool. Shape into 1-inch balls. Whisk the milk and egg in a bowl. Mix bread crumbs and cornflake crumbs in a bowl. Coat the sauerkraut balls with flour; dip in the egg mixture. Roll in the bread crumb mixture; dip in the remaining egg mixture. Coat with remaining bread crumb mixture. Fry in hot oil in a skillet until brown; drain. Serve immediately. Yield: 15 to 20 servings.

Spinach Balls

2 (10 ounces each) packages frozen chopped spinach
1 (6-ounce) package stuffing mix
1 cup grated Parmesan cheese
3/4 cup (1 1/2 sticks) butter, melted
1 small onion, chopped
6 eggs, beaten

Cook the spinach using package directions; drain. Cool for several minutes. Squeeze the excess moisture from the spinach. Combine the spinach, stuffing mix, cheese, butter, onion and eggs in a bowl and mix well. Shape into 60 bite-size balls. Arrange the balls on an ungreased baking sheet. Bake at 350 degrees in a preheated oven for 15 minutes. Serve warm. May be prepared in advance and stored, covered, in the freezer. Reheat in the microwave or oven. Yield: 60 servings.

Portage Trail Mix

1 (12-ounce) package Crispix cereal
1 (16-ounce) jar dry-roasted peanuts
1 (16-ounce) package small pretzels
2 cups packed brown sugar
1 cup (2 sticks) margarine
1/2 cup light corn syrup

Combine the cereal, peanuts and pretzels in a roasting pan and toss to mix well. Combine the brown sugar, margarine and corn syrup in saucepan. Bring to a boil, stirring occasionally. Boil for 1 1/2 minutes, stirring occasionally. Pour over the cereal mixture, stirring until coated.

Bake at 350 degrees in a preheated oven for 15 minutes, stirring 3 or 4 times. Spread the cereal mixture in a thin layer on a sheet of waxed paper. Let stand until cool. Yield: 20 to 25 servings.

Processed cereals originated in the Akron area. Ferdinand Schumacher, "the Oatmeal King" and founder of what was to be known as Quaker Oats, was from Germany. After settling in America, he missed the oatmeal he had enjoyed in his homeland and began to make small quantities for himself and his friends. When Union soldiers sampled it, they liked it so well that the orders poured in (it was tasty, inexpensive, easy to ship, and easy to store). After the Civil War, veterans still wanted their oatmeal, helping make Akron the world's largest producer of processed cereals.

"I'd rather have roses on my table than diamonds on my neck."

—*Emma Goldman*

elegant beginnings

In This Section

Sesame Artichokes

1 (14-ounce) can artichoke hearts, drained
20 melba rye or white rounds
½ cup (1 stick) butter, melted
½ teaspoon garlic powder, or to taste
Salt and freshly ground pepper to taste
Sesame seeds

Cut each artichoke heart into halves. Place each artichoke half, cut side up, on a melba round. Arrange in a single layer in a baking dish.

Drizzle the artichokes with a mixture of the butter, garlic powder, salt and pepper, allowing some of the mixture to run onto the rounds.

Bake at 350 degrees in a preheated oven for 5 minutes. Sprinkle with sesame seeds. Broil in a preheated oven for 3 minutes or until brown. Yield: 20 rounds.

The blimp has long been a symbol for Akron. The U.S. Navy's first successful blimp was built in Akron in 1917 by the Goodyear Tire and Rubber Co. In 1930, Goodyear also made the first blimp used for private commercial operation, delivered to a company in Massachusetts. More recently, The Spirit of Akron can be seen sailing high over many nationally televised sporting events.

Crab Meat on Cuke Slices

1 unpeeled large European cucumber
1 pound crab meat, shells and membranes removed
2 tablespoons undrained white horseradish
2 tablespoons nonfat mayonnaise
Juice of ½ lemon
Salt and pepper to taste

Score the surface of the cucumber with a fork. Cut into ¼-inch slices. Pat the slices with paper towels. Drain on paper towels for 20 minutes. Arrange the slices on a serving platter.

Combine the crab meat, horseradish, mayonnaise, lemon juice, salt and pepper in a bowl and mix well. Mound the crab meat mixture on the cucumber slices. Serve immediately. Do not use lump or backfin crab meat. Yield: 4 servings.

Crab Meat Canapés

1 loaf thinly sliced white bread
Butter to taste
8 ounces cream cheese, softened
8 ounces frozen crab meat, thawed, drained
2 tablespoons minced onion
2 teaspoons lemon juice, or to taste
⅛ teaspoon cayenne pepper, or to taste
Salt and black pepper to taste

Cut the bread into rounds or into other desired shapes. Arrange on a baking sheet. Toast at 375 degrees in a preheated oven until light brown on both sides, turning once. Spread lightly with butter.

Beat the cream cheese, crab meat, onion, lemon juice, cayenne pepper, salt and black pepper in a bowl until mixed. Spread the crab meat mixture on the toasted bread. Arrange on a baking sheet. Bake at 325 degrees in a preheated oven until heated through. Broil in a preheated oven until brown and bubbly. Serve immediately. May spread the crab meat mixture on untoasted rounds. Yield: 24 servings.

Cheddar Crab Canapés

6 ounces crab meat
1 cup shredded Cheddar cheese
1/4 cup minced onion
1 tablespoon minced fresh parsley
1 cup mayonnaise
1 loaf French bread, thinly sliced
Paprika to taste

Combine the crab meat, cheese, onion and parsley in a bowl and
mix well. Stir in the mayonnaise. Spread the crab meat mixture
on 1 side of each bread slice. Arrange bread slices, filling side up,
in a single layer on a baking sheet. Sprinkle with paprika. Broil in
a preheated oven for 5 to 6 minutes or until bubbly. Cut into
bite-size pieces if desired. Yield: 20 servings.

Goat Cheese Crostini

8 ounces goat cheese
1/4 cup crushed macadamia nuts or pistachios, toasted
2 tablespoons extra-virgin olive oil
2 tablespoons chopped sun-dried tomatoes
1 tablespoon cracked pepper
1 teaspoon salt
1 teaspoon sugar
1 baguette French bread, cut diagonally into 1/2-inch
    slices, toasted
24 macadamia nuts or pistachios

Combine the goat cheese, macadamia nuts, olive oil, sun-dried
tomatoes, pepper, salt and sugar in a bowl and mix well. Spread
the goat cheese mixture on the bread slices just before serving.
Top each crostini with a macadamia nut or pistachio.
Yield: 24 crostini.

In parts of Italy, serving crostini, or "little crusts," is considered a sign of hospitality. These small toasts, drizzled with olive oil and topped with such foods as olives or sun-dried tomatoes, began as a creative way to use bread left over from yesterday's loaf.

Mozzarella and Tomato Crostini

1 baguette French bread, cut into 1-inch slices
2 to 3 tablespoons butter, softened
10 ounces mozzarella cheese, sliced
3 ripe plum tomatoes, thinly sliced
1 tablespoon olive oil
Oregano and basil to taste
Salt and freshly ground pepper to taste
Anchovy fillets (optional)

Spread 1 side of each bread slice with some of the butter. Arrange the bread slices butter side up on a baking sheet. Top each with a slice of the cheese.

Arrange the tomatoes in a shallow dish. Drizzle with the olive oil. Sprinkle with the oregano, basil, salt and pepper and toss gently to coat. Top each crostini with a tomato slice. Bake at 350 degrees in a preheated oven for 10 minutes or until heated through and bubbly. Garnish with sprigs of fresh basil. Serve immediately. Add anchovy fillets if desired. Yield: 12 to 15 crostini.

Mushroom Canapés

Thinly sliced bread
3 ounces cream cheese, softened
1 (3-ounce) can mushrooms, drained, finely chopped
2 tablespoons mayonnaise
½ small onion, finely chopped
Paprika
Sprigs of fresh parsley

Trim crusts from bread. Cut into 48 rounds. Combine the cream cheese, mushrooms, mayonnaise and onion in a bowl and mix well. Spread the mushroom mixture on the bread rounds.

Arrange the rounds on a baking sheet. Broil in a preheated oven for 2 to 3 minutes or until puffy and light brown. Sprinkle with paprika and top with a sprig of fresh parsley. Yield: 48 canapés.

Hot Mushroom Canapés

2 loaves thinly sliced white bread, crusts trimmed
1 medium onion, finely chopped
1 tablespoon margarine
12 ounces fresh mushrooms, chopped
Salt and pepper to taste
12 ounces cream cheese, softened
1 teaspoon Worcestershire sauce
1/2 teaspoon garlic powder
1/2 to 1 cup (1 to 2 sticks) margarine, melted

Roll the bread slices thin on a hard surface. Sauté the onion
in 1 tablespoon margarine in a skillet until tender. Add the
mushrooms and mix well. Sauté for 5 minutes. Remove from
heat. Season with salt and pepper. Add the cream cheese and
mix well. Stir in the Worcestershire sauce and garlic powder.

Spread each bread slice with 1 tablespoon of the cream cheese
mixture. Roll to enclose the filling. Cut into bite-size slices. May
freeze at this point. Arrange the slices on a baking sheet. Brush
1 side of each slice with some of the melted margarine. Broil in a
preheated oven until light brown. Serve immediately.
Yield: variable.

Swiss Canapé Broil

1 cup shredded Swiss cheese
1 (3-ounce) can sliced mushrooms, drained
1/3 cup chopped pepperoni
1/4 cup chopped onion
2 tablespoons chopped black olives
1/3 cup mayonnaise
Toasted bread squares or Triscuits

Combine the cheese, mushrooms, pepperoni, onion and black
olives in a bowl and mix well. Stir in the mayonnaise. Spread the
cheese mixture on the bread squares. Arrange the squares on a
baking sheet. Broil 3 inches from the heat source in a preheated
oven until bubbly. Serve immediately. Yield: variable.

*The sport of professional
bowling had its
beginnings in Akron.
The Professional Bowlers
Association was founded
in Akron by the late Eddie
Elias. The first PBA
tournament was held in
1962. Three years later,
Elias launched The
Tournament of Champions
in Akron. The tournament
boasted a $100,000 prize
fund, something unheard
of in bowling at the time.*

Black Olive Hors d'Oeuvres

1 package English muffins, split
1 1/2 cups shredded sharp Cheddar cheese
1/2 cup chopped black olives
1/2 cup chopped scallions
1/2 cup mayonnaise
1/2 teaspoon curry powder
Salt to taste

Arrange the muffin halves cut side up on a baking sheet. Broil in a preheated oven until light brown. Cut each half into 5 to 6 wedges with kitchen shears. Combine the cheese, black olives and scallions in a bowl and mix well. Stir in the mayonnaise, curry powder and salt.

Spread the olive mixture on the muffin wedges. Arrange the wedges on a baking sheet. Broil for 1 minute or until bubbly. Serve immediately. May prepare olive mixture 1 day in advance and store, covered, in the refrigerator. Prepare the muffin wedges 1 day in advance and store in sealable plastic bags.
Yield: 60 to 72 wedges.

Parmesan Onion Canapés

1 cup mayonnaise
1 cup grated Parmesan cheese
1/2 cup finely chopped onion or scallions
1 tablespoon milk
1 loaf sliced party bread, lightly toasted

Combine the mayonnaise, cheese, onion and milk in a bowl and mix well. Spread the cheese mixture on the toasted bread. Arrange the slices on a baking sheet. Broil 4 inches from the heat source in a preheated oven for 2 to 3 minutes or until bubbly and golden brown. Serve immediately. Yield: 36 canapés.

Scotch Salmon Canapés

8 ounces cream cheese, softened
8 ounces smoked salmon, chopped
2 tablespoons Scotch whiskey
2 teaspoons lemon juice
1/2 teaspoon prepared white horseradish
1/8 to 1/4 teaspoon cayenne pepper
32 slices European cucumbers
2 tablespoons chopped fresh chives (optional)

Combine the cream cheese, salmon, whiskey, lemon juice,
horseradish and cayenne pepper in a food processor container.
Process until blended. Spoon onto the cucumber slices. Sprinkle
with the chives. May blend the chives with the cream cheese
mixture. Yield: 32 canapés.

The photograph for this recipe appears on the cover.

Sun-Dried Tomato Canapés

3 ounces sun-dried tomatoes
1 cup white wine vinegar
2/3 cup olive oil
7 garlic cloves, minced
2 tablespoons grated Parmesan cheese
1 tablespoon white wine
1 teaspoon basil
1/2 teaspoon oregano
1/4 teaspoon each thyme, parsley flakes and marjoram
Toast points, crackers or bread rounds

Soak the sun-dried tomatoes in the wine vinegar in a bowl for
1 hour or until softened; drain. Cut finely with kitchen shears.
Combine the olive oil, garlic, cheese, wine, basil, oregano, thyme,
parsley flakes and marjoram in a bowl and mix well. Stir in the
sun-dried tomatoes. Chill, covered, for 24 hours. Spoon the sun-
dried tomato mixture onto toast points, crackers or bread rounds
just before serving. May also be heated and served over hot,
cooked pasta. Yield: variable.

*"There are persons of
capricious appetites who
could make a full meal
of these adventurous
appetisers; Rossini even
found inspiration in
them for he composed a
phantasy on the 'Four
Hors D'oeuvres' (butter,
radishes, anchovies and
pickled gherkins)."*

—*from* Good Cheer:
The Romance of Food
and Feasting

Très Facile Canapés

8 ounces port wine cheese spread
1/3 cup chopped black or green olives
1/2 teaspoon dry mustard
1/8 teaspoon pepper
1/3 cup mayonnaise
Melba toast rounds or party rye bread

Combine the cheese spread, olives, dry mustard and pepper in a
bowl and mix well. Stir in the mayonnaise. Spread the cheese
mixture on the melba toast. Arrange the rounds on a baking sheet.
Bake at 450 degrees in a preheated oven for 5 minutes or until
bubbly. Yield: variable.

Anchovy Celery Dip

8 ounces cream cheese, softened
3 tablespoons cream
1 tablespoon minced onion
1 tablespoon lemon juice
1 tablespoon anchovy paste
1/2 teaspoon celery seeds
1/8 teaspoon paprika
Potato chips or assorted party crackers

Beat the cream cheese and cream in a mixing bowl until creamy,
scraping the bowl occasionally. Stir in the onion, lemon juice,
anchovy paste, celery seeds and paprika. Chill, covered, for several
hours before serving. Serve with potato chips or assorted party
crackers. Substitute reduced-fat cream cheese for the cream cheese
and delete the cream for a reduction in fat grams.
Yield: 16 to 20 servings.

Hot Crab and Shrimp Dip

16 ounces cream cheese, softened
2 (4 ounces each) cans lump crab meat, drained, rinsed,
    shells removed
4 ounces peeled cooked shrimp, finely chopped
2 or 3 green onions, chopped
1/2 cup mayonnaise
1/4 cup dry white wine
1 large garlic clove, minced
2 teaspoons Dijon mustard
2 teaspoons confectioners' sugar
1 teaspoon seasoned salt
1/2 teaspoon salt, or to taste
1/4 teaspoon cayenne pepper
1 baguette French bread, thinly sliced, toasted

Combine the cream cheese, crab meat, shrimp and green onions
in a bowl and mix well. Stir in the mayonnaise, white wine,
garlic, Dijon mustard, confectioners' sugar, seasoned salt, salt
and cayenne pepper. Spoon into a 1- to 1½-quart baking dish.

Bake at 350 degrees in a preheated oven for 30 minutes or until
bubbly. Cool slightly. Serve warm with toasted bread slices and/or
melba toast. May be prepared in advance and stored, covered, in
the refrigerator. Bake just before serving. May also spread the dip
on crostini and broil in a preheated oven until bubbly for an
individual hors d'oeuvre. Yield: 12 servings.

Puréed roasted eggplant is known as "poor man's caviar" because it is economical yet very rich in taste. In the Middle East, the spread is known as baba ganoujh, or "harem girl."

Eggplant Dip with Country Bread

3 pounds eggplant (about 2 or 3 eggplant)
4 tablespoons olive oil
5 scallion bulbs, thinly sliced
1 medium red bell pepper, finely chopped
1/2 small jalapeño chile, seeded, minced, or
    1/8 teaspoon cayenne pepper
4 ounces mushrooms, thinly sliced
1 large tomato, peeled, seeded, finely chopped
1/3 cup fresh basil leaves, finely chopped
2 1/2 tablespoons finely minced chives
2 teaspoons minced garlic
Salt and freshly ground pepper to taste
2 small loaves country bread, cut into cubes

Cut the eggplant lengthwise into halves. Brush with 1 tablespoon
of the olive oil. Arrange the eggplant halves, cut side down, on
a baking sheet. Bake at 350 degrees in a preheated oven for
45 minutes or until the peel is wrinkled and the pulp is tender
to the touch when pierced with a fork. Let stand until cool.

Heat 1 tablespoon of the olive oil in a skillet over medium heat.
Add the scallions, red pepper and jalapeño chile and mix well.
Cook for 5 minutes or until tender, stirring occasionally. Spoon
the red pepper mixture into a bowl. Add the mushrooms to the
skillet. Cook for 5 to 7 minutes or until the moisture has been
absorbed and the mushrooms are tender, stirring frequently. Let
stand until cool.

Scoop the eggplant flesh onto a work surface and finely chop;
discard the peel. Chop the mushrooms. Stir the eggplant and
mushrooms into the red pepper mixture. Add the tomato, basil,
chives, 1 1/2 teaspoons of the garlic and the remaining 2 tablespoons
olive oil. May be prepared to this point up to 1 day in advance
and stored, covered, in the refrigerator. Season with salt and
pepper. Spoon into a serving bowl. Sprinkle with additional
chopped fresh chives.

Toss the bread cubes with the remaining 1/2 teaspoon garlic in a
bowl. Spread the cubes in a single layer on a baking sheet. Bake at
400 degrees in a preheated oven for 10 minutes or until golden
brown, turning once. Serve with the dip. Yield: 12 to 15 servings.

Roasted Garlic and Pepper Dip

2 large garlic bulbs, tops removed
1 red bell pepper
1 cup reduced-fat sour cream
3/4 teaspoon salt
1/4 teaspoon freshly ground pepper
2 pounds carrots, sliced
3 heads Belgian endive
1 pound jicama, sliced
3 or 4 red or yellow bell peppers
2 European cucumbers, sliced
2 pounds smoked trout or salmon, cut into 1-inch pieces
2 pounds cooked medium shrimp, peeled, deveined
Assorted party crackers

Place the garlic in a small baking dish. Roast at 350 degrees in a preheated oven for 45 minutes or until tender. Transfer to a wire rack to cool. Arrange 1 red pepper on a broiler rack in a broiler pan. Broil 5 inches from the heat source in a preheated oven for 20 minutes or until the skin is charred and blistered, turning every 5 minutes; cover. Let stand until cool. Peel, seed and chop the red pepper.

Squeeze the garlic from the skins and measure 3 tablespoons. Combine 3 tablespoons garlic pulp, roasted red pepper, sour cream, salt and pepper in a food processor container. Process until puréed. Spoon into a serving bowl. Serve with the carrots, endive, jicama, bell peppers, cucumbers, trout, shrimp and/or assorted party crackers.

The flavor of the dip is enhanced if prepared one day in advance and stored, covered, in the refrigerator. May substitute 1/2 cup drained rinsed commercially prepared roasted red bell peppers for the fresh red bell pepper. Yield: 1 1/2 cups.

Garlic once formed part of the rations of the Egyptian pyramid builders and was also given to Roman soldiers to invigorate them.

Basil Parmesan Spread

1 cup loosely packed chopped fresh spinach
1 cup chopped fresh basil
1 tablespoon minced garlic
1 cup grated Parmesan cheese
1/4 cup olive oil
Salt and pepper to taste
8 ounces reduced-fat cream cheese, softened
4 ounces feta cheese
1/4 cup chopped oil-packed sun-dried tomatoes
Water crackers or sliced crusty Italian bread

Line a 3-cup mold or rectangular dish with plastic wrap,
allowing overhang. Combine the spinach, basil and garlic in a
food processor container. Process until puréed. Add the Parmesan
cheese, olive oil and salt and pepper, processing constantly until
blended. Combine the cream cheese and feta cheese in a bowl
and mix well.

Layer 1/3 of the cream cheese mixture, 1/2 of the spinach mixture
and 1/2 of the sun-dried tomatoes in the prepared mold. Top with
1/2 of the cream cheese mixture, the remaining spinach mixture and
the remaining sun-dried tomatoes. Spread with the remaining
cream cheese mixture; press lightly. Cover with the plastic
overhang. Chill for 8 to 10 hours. Invert onto a serving platter.
Garnish with sprigs of fresh parsley. Serve with water crackers or
crusty Italian bread. Yield 8 servings.

Brie in a Sack

1 (17-ounce) package frozen puff pastry, thawed
2 (4 ounces each) rounds Brie cheese
1/4 cup apricot preserves
1/4 cup chopped pecans
1 egg yolk, lightly beaten
Assorted party crackers

Unfold one sheet of the pastry on a lightly floured surface. Roll the pastry large enough to enclose 1 Brie round with enough overhang to gather like a sack. Place 1 round in the middle of the pastry. Spread the round with half the preserves and sprinkle with half the pecans. Gather the edges of the pastry over the round to resemble a sack and tie with cotton twine.

Place the sack on a lightly greased baking sheet. Repeat the process with the remaining pastry, Brie cheese, preserves and pecans. Chill for 1 hour. Brush the sacks with the egg yolk.

Bake at 400 degrees in a preheated oven for 25 to 30 minutes or until golden brown and puffed. Reduce the oven temperature to 350 degrees if the pastry browns too quickly. Serve warm or at room temperature with assorted party crackers. Yield: 12 servings.

"I am beginning to think that it is the sweet, simple things of life which are the real ones after all."

—*Laura Ingalls Wilder*

Bridge Street Brie

1 sheet frozen puff pastry
¼ cup (½ stick) butter
6 tablespoons finely chopped shallots
1 pound mushrooms, coarsely chopped
¼ cup flour
2 cups heavy cream
1 (2-pound) round Brie cheese
2 egg yolks, lightly beaten
Assorted party crackers

Thaw the pastry for 1 hour or until at room temperature. Heat the butter in a skillet until melted. Add the shallots. Cook for 5 minutes or until tender, stirring constantly. Stir in the mushrooms. Cook for 15 minutes or until the moisture is absorbed, stirring frequently. Remove from heat. Stir in the flour. Add the heavy cream and mix well. Bring to a boil, stirring constantly. Cook until thickened, stirring frequently. Let stand until at room temperature.

Roll the pastry large enough to completely cover the Brie, allowing enough overhang to gather like a sack. Place the Brie in the center of the pastry. Spoon the mushroom mixture over the top of the Brie, allowing some of the mixture to drizzle over the edge. Gather the edges of the pastry over the Brie to resemble a sack and twist so the edges hang down artfully. Brush the entire surface of the pastry with the egg yolks.

Arrange on a baking sheet sprayed with nonstick cooking spray. Bake at 450 degrees in a preheated oven for 10 minutes. Reduce the oven temperature to 350 degrees. Bake for 10 minutes longer. Serve with assorted party crackers. May be stored, covered with plastic wrap, in the refrigerator for up to 4 days or frozen for future use before baking. Let stand at room temperature for 20 to 30 minutes before baking. Yield: 20 servings.

Baked Caramel Cinnamon Brie

½ cup (1 stick) butter
½ cup packed brown sugar
⅓ cup sugar
½ cup heavy cream
¼ teaspoon nutmeg
¼ teaspoon cinnamon
1 (12-ounce) round Brie cheese
2 tablespoons sliced almonds, toasted
1 baguette French bread, thinly sliced

Combine the butter, brown sugar and sugar in a saucepan. Cook over low heat until the butter melts and the sugars dissolve, stirring frequently. Add the heavy cream gradually, stirring constantly. Stir in the nutmeg and cinnamon. Cook until thickened, stirring constantly.

Place the Brie in a round baking pan. Drizzle the brown sugar mixture over the top of the Brie. Bake at 225 degrees in a preheated oven for 10 minutes or until the Brie is heated through. Remove from oven. Sprinkle with the almonds. Let stand for 5 to 10 minutes before serving. Garnish with fresh strawberries and/or Golden Delicious or Granny Smith apple slices. Serve with the sliced bread. Yield: 8 to 10 servings.

"Before the beginning of great balance, there must be chaos. Before a brilliant person begins something great, they must look foolish in the crowd."

—from the I Ching

Caramelized Brie

1 (8- to 10-ounce) round Brie cheese, chilled
1 (11-ounce) can French bread dough
¼ cup chopped pecans
1 tablespoon brown sugar
Assorted party crackers

Place the Brie on a baking sheet sprayed with nonstick cooking spray. Wrap the bread dough in a ring around the Brie, twisting in a spiral as you wrap; press the ends together to seal. Make 1-inch slits in the dough at 2-inch intervals with kitchen shears. Sprinkle the top of the Brie with the pecans and brown sugar.

Bake at 350 degrees in a preheated oven for 30 minutes. Let stand for 20 to 60 minutes before serving. Cut into wedges. Serve with assorted party crackers.

For a different presentation, cut the bread dough into halves. Roll each half into a slender rope and braid. Wrap the braid around the Brie. Yield: 5 to 10 servings.

Mock Boursin au Poivre

8 ounces cream cheese, softened
1 garlic clove, crushed
1 teaspoon caraway seeds
1 teaspoon basil
1 teaspoon dillweed
1 teaspoon chopped chives
Lemon pepper to taste
Assorted party crackers

Combine the cream cheese, garlic, caraway seeds, basil, dillweed and chives in a bowl and mix well. Shape into a round disc or into a log, 2 inches thick. Coat all sides generously with lemon pepper. Serve with assorted party crackers. Yield: 16 servings.

Curried Chicken Liver Pâté

½ cup (1 stick) butter
1 pound chicken livers
2 medium onions, chopped
1 teaspoon paprika
1 teaspoon curry powder
1 teaspoon salt
½ teaspoon pepper
¼ cup (½ stick) butter, softened
Party rye or pumpernickel bread
Sweet pickles

Heat ½ cup butter in a skillet until melted. Add the chicken livers, onions, paprika, curry powder, salt and pepper and mix well. Cook just until the livers are barely pink, stirring frequently. Remove from heat. Drain off approximately ½ cup of the liquid.

Process ¼ cup butter in a food processor until creamy. Add the liver mixture. Process for 10 seconds or until smooth; mixture will be very thin. Pour into a crock or onion-soup casserole. Chill, covered, for 8 to 10 hours. Serve with party rye or pumpernickel bread and sweet pickles. Yield: 4 servings.

Nationally recognized artist Don Drumm calls Akron home. His gallery near the University of Akron has become the largest showcase of American arts and crafts between New York and Chicago.

Chicken Terrine

2 teaspoons unflavored gelatin
1 (14-ounce) can chicken consommé
1 (5-ounce) can chicken, drained
1 small onion, chopped
3 ounces cream cheese, softened
1 tablespoon mayonnaise
1/4 teaspoon salt
1/4 teaspoon pepper
1/4 teaspoon thyme
Assorted party crackers

Soften the gelatin in a small amount of the consommé in a bowl.
Heat the remaining consommé in a saucepan; do not boil. Remove
from heat. Add the gelatin mixture, stirring until dissolved. Rinse
a small mold with cold water. Add half the consommé mixture.
Chill until set.

Process the chicken and onion in a food processor until ground.
Add the cream cheese, mayonnaise, salt, pepper and thyme.
Process until blended. Spoon over the prepared layer. Pour the
remaining consommé mixture over the top. Chill for 15 minutes
or until set. Invert onto a serving platter. Garnish with fresh herbs
and/or edible flowers. Serve with assorted party crackers.
Yield: 6 servings.

Herbed Gouda Spread

8 ounces Gouda cheese, shredded
1/2 cup sour cream
1 tablespoon Italian salad dressing mix
Assorted party crackers
Sliced apples

Combine the cheese, sour cream and dressing mix in a mixer bowl.
Beat until blended, scraping the bowl occasionally. Chill, covered,
until serving time. Serve with assorted party crackers and sliced
apples. Yield: 1 1/4 cups.

French Herb Cheese

2 cups nonfat yogurt
8 ounces reduced-fat small curd cottage cheese
1½ tablespoons extra-virgin olive oil
4 teaspoons minced garlic
1 tablespoon white wine vinegar or rice wine vinegar
1 tablespoon fresh lemon juice, or to taste
Salt and freshly ground pepper to taste
½ cup finely chopped fresh herbs
Assorted party crackers
Assorted crudités

Drain the yogurt in a yogurt funnel or cheesecloth-lined colander in the refrigerator for 2 hours. Drain the cottage cheese in a fine mesh strainer in the refrigerator for 2 hours. Process the yogurt and cottage cheese in a food processor until puréed. Add the olive oil, garlic, wine vinegar, lemon juice, salt and pepper. Process until blended.

Adjust the seasonings, adding additional lemon juice, salt and pepper if desired. Stir in the herbs. Spoon into a serving bowl. Chill, covered, for 2 to 3 hours to allow the flavors to marry. Serve with assorted party crackers and/or assorted crudités.
Yield: 8 servings.

Ice skating legend and Junior League of Akron member Carol Heiss Jenkins calls Akron her home. In the 1950s and 1960s, she won every leading amateur title for women's figure skating—the National Championship, the World Championship, and the Olympic Championship. She came to Akron in the early 1960s with her husband, attorney Hayes Alan Jenkins, a gold medalist skater in the 1956 Olympics.

Luscious Layered Pesto Spread

8 ounces cream cheese, softened
1 cup (2 sticks) unsalted butter, softened
3/4 cup freshly grated Parmesan cheese
1/4 cup fresh basil leaves
3 tablespoons olive oil
1/4 cup chopped pine nuts
Salt and pepper to taste
1 baguette French bread, sliced

Combine the cream cheese and butter in a food processor container. Process until smooth and set aside. Process the Parmesan cheese, basil and olive oil in an empy clean food processor until of a paste consistency. Add the pine nuts, salt and pepper. Process until blended.

Moisten two 2-foot squares of cheesecloth with water and wring dry. Lay the squares flat, one on top of the other. Line a 2 1/2-cup loaf pan or any straight-sided mold with the cheesecloth, allowing an overhang. Spread 1/6 of the cream cheese mixture in the prepared pan. Spread with 1/5 of the pesto mixture. Repeat the layers until all of the ingredients are used, ending with the cream cheese mixture. Fold the ends of the cheesecloth over the top and press lightly. Chill for 1 1/2 hours or until firm; do not allow to remain in pan more than 1 1/2 hours. Invert onto a serving platter. Garnish with sprigs of fresh basil. Serve with bread slices.
Yield: 7 to 8 servings.

Cocktail Party Shrimp

2 cups cooked shrimp, drained, finely chopped
8 ounces cream cheese, softened
1 medium onion, grated
1/2 (20-ounce) bottle catsup
Prepared horseradish to taste
Butter crackers

Combine the first five ingredients in a bowl and mix well. Chill, covered, until serving time. Garnish with sprigs of fresh parsley. Serve with butter crackers. Yield: 6 to 8 servings.

Vegetarian White Bean Pâté

1/2 red onion, chopped
2 ribs celery, chopped
2 garlic cloves, minced
2 tablespoons olive oil
1 (15-ounce) can cannellini beans, drained, rinsed
1 egg
1/4 cup fine bread crumbs
1/4 cup heavy cream
1/4 cup chopped drained oil-packed sun-dried tomatoes
1/4 cup dry white wine
3 tablespoons chopped fresh parsley
1 tablespoon chopped fresh sage
Salt and pepper to taste
Toast points, assorted party breads or party crackers

Sauté the onion, celery and garlic in the olive oil in a skillet until tender. Purée the beans and egg in a food processor until smooth. Combine the onion mixture, bean mixture, bread crumbs, heavy cream, sun-dried tomatoes, white wine, parsley, sage, salt and pepper in a bowl and mix well. Spoon the bean mixture into a 9-inch round baking dish. Top with parchment paper and cover with foil.

Bake at 400 degrees in a preheated oven for 45 minutes or until the center is set. Remove to a wire rack to cool. Weight down the pâté with a plate. Let stand for 45 minutes. Serve warm or at room temperature. Garnish with fresh sage leaves or arrange the sage leaves in a design over the top of the pâté before baking. Serve with toast points, party breads and/or assorted party crackers. Yield: 10 to 12 servings.

The spirit of invention is a strong part of this community. Akron has been home to the National Inventors Hall of Fame since 1987. The museum and home of the Hall of Fame, called "Inventure Place," opened in down-town Akron in 1995.

Aïoli Platter

12 small artichokes, trimmed
8 ounces snow peas, trimmed
1 pound carrots, peeled, cut into 2-inch pieces
3 pounds cauliflower, cut into florets
1 pound carpaccio (thin shavings of uncooked beef)
2 recipes Aïoli Sauce
7 pounds cod, poached
1 pound chick-peas, cooked
3 large red or green bell peppers, sliced
1 pint cherry tomatoes, rinsed, stems left intact
1 pound zucchini, sliced
1 pound small potatoes, boiled, peeled
6 eggs, hard-cooked, cut into halves horizontally
1/4 cup capers
1/2 cup chopped parsley

Boil the artichokes in water to cover in a saucepan until tender;
drain well. Remove and discard the chokes. Blanch the snow peas
by plunging briefly into boiling water, then into cold water.
Blanch the carrots and cauliflower in the same fashion. Place a
small amount of the beef at a time between sheets of waxed paper
and pound with a heavy saucepan to smooth out irregularities.
Spoon Aïoli Sauce into the center of each artichoke. Place
1 artichoke in the center of each individual plate. Arrange cod,
carpaccio, vegetables and eggs in spoke fashion around the
artichokes. Sprinkle with capers and parsley. Yield: 12 servings.

Aïoli Sauce

8 to 10 garlic cloves, peeled
2 egg yolks, at room temperature, lightly beaten
Salt and freshly ground white pepper to taste
Juice of 1 lemon
1 teaspoon Dijon mustard
3/4 cup each peanut oil and olive oil, at room temperature

Purée the garlic in a food processor or blender. Add the egg yolks.
Season with salt and pepper. Add the lemon juice and mustard.
Process until a smooth paste forms. Add the peanut oil and olive
oil in a steady stream with the food processor running. Process
until sauce is thick and shiny. Chill, covered, until needed.
Yield: 1 3/4 cups.

Antipasto Platter

Florets of 1 head cauliflower
2 pounds carrots, peeled, diagonally sliced
Florets of 1 bunch broccoli
2 (14 ounces each) cans artichoke hearts, drained, cut into halves
1 (5-ounce) jar pimento-stuffed green olives, drained
1 (6-ounce) jar black olives, drained
1 cup white vinegar
1/4 cup sugar
1 tablespoon dry mustard
1 1/2 tablespoons Italian seasoning
1 1/2 teaspoons salt
1 1/2 cups olive oil
Lettuce leaves
1 red bell pepper

Place the cauliflower, carrots, broccoli, artichokes, green olives and black olives in separate sealable plastic bags. Whisk the vinegar, sugar, dry mustard, Italian seasoning and salt in a saucepan. Bring to a boil over medium heat, stirring constantly. Remove from heat. Stir in the olive oil.

Pour some of the olive oil mixture into each plastic bag and seal tightly. Toss to coat. Marinate in the refrigerator for 8 to 10 hours, turning occasionally; drain.

Arrange the lettuce leaves on a large serving platter. Hollow out the red pepper, discarding the seeds and membranes. Place the red pepper in the center of the platter. Spoon the black olives into the red pepper. Arrange the cauliflower, carrots, broccoli, green olives and artichokes around the red pepper. Yield: 25 servings.

The Jacobs brothers, Richard and the late David, grew up in Akron. The two amassed a multi-million dollar empire of holdings that included shopping malls, office buildings, and the Cleveland Indians baseball team. Indeed, the stadium, Jacobs Field, bears their name.

Cheese Board

Soft-ripened cheeses, such as
    Brie
    Saint André
    Explorateur
Firm cheeses such as
    Huntsman
    England's Choice
Semi-soft cheeses such as
    Holland's Crème de Polder
    Morbier
Assorted party crackers

To serve 10 guests, select one 8-ounce portion of a soft cheese, a hard cheese and a semi-soft cheese (a total of 24 ounces). Garnish the serving tray with red and green grapes, sliced strawberries and/or grape leaves brushed with olive oil. Fan out the strawberry slices attractively.

To serve 25 guests, select three 1-pound portions of each of the above types of cheeses. Add another soft-ripened cheese such as a 1-pound layered Brie. Serve with assorted party crackers.
Yield: 10 to 25 servings.

Almond-Stuffed Olives

72 large pimento-stuffed Spanish olives
72 blanched whole almonds
¼ cup olive oil
¼ teaspoon crushed red pepper flakes
1 teaspoon oregano
1 garlic clove, minced

Remove the pimentos from the olives. Stuff each olive with an almond. Place the olives in a bowl. Combine the olive oil, red pepper flakes, oregano and garlic in a bowl and mix well. Pour over the olives, tossing to coat. Marinate, covered, in the refrigerator for 1 to 2 days, stirring occasionally. Yield: 72 olives.

Snow Peas with Boursin

60 snow peas, trimmed, strings removed
5 ounces boursin, softened

Blanch the peas in boiling water in a saucepan for 30 seconds; drain. Plunge the peas into ice water immediately; drain. Slit open the straight seam of each pea with a small sharp knife. Pipe the cheese into each pea using a pastry tube fitted with a small tip. Arrange on a serving platter. Garnish with fresh herbs. Yield: 60 servings.

The photograph for this recipe appears on the cover.

Olives are among the earliest of documented appetizers. Olives were used as a first course in ancient Rome and were also served between courses to cleanse the palate.

Shrimp-Stuffed Endive

3 cups water
8 ounces unpeeled medium shrimp
1/3 cup cream cheese, softened
1 tablespoon chili sauce
1/2 teaspoon sugar
1/2 teaspoon lemon juice
1/4 teaspoon salt
2 drops of hot pepper sauce
1 (8-ounce) can water chestnuts, drained, finely chopped
1/3 cup chopped seeded cucumber
1 tablespoon thinly sliced green onions
4 heads endive, separated into spears

Bring the water to a boil in a saucepan. Add the shrimp. Boil for 3 to 5 minutes or until the shrimp turn pink. Drain and rinse with cold water. Peel, devein and chop the shrimp.

Combine the cream cheese, chili sauce, sugar, lemon juice, salt and hot pepper sauce in a mixing bowl. Beat at medium speed until smooth, scraping the bowl occasionally. Stir in the shrimp, water chestnuts, cucumber and green onions. Chill, covered, in the refrigerator.

Spoon 1 tablespoon of the shrimp mixture onto the stem end of each endive spear. Arrange in a decorative pattern on a serving platter. Yield: 32 servings.

Asparagus Bites

30 thin fresh asparagus spears
10 slices white bread, crusts trimmed
10 slices whole wheat bread, crusts trimmed
10 slices pumpernickel, crusts trimmed
8 ounces cream cheese, softened
3 ounces Gorgonzola cheese, softened
1 egg
3/4 cup (1 1/4 sticks) butter, melted

Trim the asparagus spears the same length as the bread slices. Place the asparagus in a large skillet. Add just enough water to cover. Bring to a boil. Boil for 3 to 5 minutes or until tender-crisp; drain. Rinse with cold water; drain.

Roll the bread on a hard surface with a rolling pin until flattened. Beat the cream cheese, Gorgonzola cheese and egg in a mixing bowl until smooth, scraping the bowl occasionally. Spread the cheese mixture on 1 side of each bread slice. Place 1 asparagus spear on the edge of each bread slice and roll to enclose the filling. Dip the rolls in the butter until coated.

Arrange seam side down on a baking sheet lined with waxed paper. Freeze for 2 hours or until firm. Cut each roll into 3 equal portions. May freeze for future use at this point. Arrange the slices on a baking sheet. Bake at 400 degrees in a preheated oven for 15 minutes or until golden brown. Yield: 90 servings.

"Hors d'oeuvres have always held a pathetic interest for me," said Reginald. "They remind me of one's childhood that one goes through, wondering what the next course is going to be like—and during the rest of the menu, one wishes one had eaten more of the hors d'oeuvres."

—Reginald at the Carlton

Saki (Hector Hugh Munro) (1870-1916)

Asparagus with Herbed Cheese

1 pound fresh asparagus spears
8 ounces Vidalia onions or other sweet onions, thickly sliced
1 cup part-skim ricotta cheese
2 tablespoons chopped fresh chervil
2 tablespoons chopped fresh chives
2 tablespoons chopped fresh thyme
1 baguette sourdough bread
1 tablespoon extra-virgin olive oil
1/4 teaspoon salt
1/4 teaspoon pepper
Sprigs of fresh parsley

Snap off the tough ends of the asparagus. Cut each spear into
1-inch pieces. Remove the scales with a knife or vegetable peeler
if desired. Bring enough water to cover the asparagus and onions
to a boil in a saucepan. Add the asparagus and onions. Boil for
3 minutes; drain. Plunge the vegetables into ice water in a bowl;
drain. Pat dry with paper towels.

Combine the ricotta cheese, chervil, chives and thyme in a bowl
and mix well. Cut six 1-inch slices from the baguette, reserving
the remaining bread for another use. Arrange the slices on a
baking sheet sprayed with nonstick cooking spray. Toast at
400 degrees in a preheated oven or broil until brown on both
sides. Spread with the cheese mixture.

Heat the olive oil in a nonstick skillet. Add the onion, salt and
pepper and mix well. Sauté for 4 minutes or until the onion is
light brown. Add the asparagus. Sauté just until heated through.
Layer the vegetable mixture over the cheese. Arrange on a baking
sheet. Broil in a preheated oven just until heated through. Top
each slice with a sprig of parsley. Yield: 6 servings.

Bacon-Wrapped Water Chestnuts

1 (1-pound) package bacon
2 (8 ounces each) cans whole water chestnuts, drained
1/2 cup catsup
1/4 cup packed brown sugar
Soy sauce to taste

Cut the bacon slices into thirds. Wrap each water chestnut with
1/3 slice and secure with a wooden pick. Arrange on a baking
sheet. Combine the catsup, brown sugar and soy sauce in a bowl
and mix well. Drizzle over the water chestnuts. Bake at 350
degrees in a preheated oven for 30 minutes. Yield: 6 to 8 servings.

Marinated Brussels Sprouts

1 1/4 pounds brussels sprouts, trimmed
Salt to taste
1/4 cup olive oil
2 teaspoons parsley flakes
1 teaspoon grated lemon zest
1/2 teaspoon sugar
1/4 teaspoon garlic powder
1/4 teaspoon salt
1/4 teaspoon tarragon
1/8 teaspoon pepper
3 tablespoons lemon juice
2 tablespoons white wine vinegar

Cut the brussels sprouts into halves. Cook in boiling salted water
in a saucepan for 5 minutes or until tender but bright green;
drain. Spoon into a bowl.

Combine the olive oil, parsley flakes, lemon zest, sugar, garlic
powder, salt, tarragon and pepper in a separate bowl and mix well.
Pour the olive oil mixture over the sprouts and toss to coat. Chill,
covered, for 2 to 10 hours, stirring occasionally. Drizzle with the
lemon juice and wine vinegar just before serving. Spoon into a
serving bowl. Serve with wooden picks. Yield: 6 to 8 servings.

Capers are the unopened buds of a shrub that grows wild in India, northwest Africa, and the Mediterranean.

Caponata in Lavash Cups

1 (12-ounce) eggplant
1/2 yellow bell pepper
1/2 red bell pepper
1 onion, finely chopped
1 large garlic clove, minced
1/4 cup water
2 tablespoons fresh lemon juice
1 tablespoon brown sugar
1 teaspoon salt
1/4 cup golden raisins
2 tablespoons drained capers
2 tablespoons chopped fresh flat-leaf parsley
1/2 teaspoon anise seeds
1 (16- to 18-inch) round thin pliable lavash
1/2 teaspoon kosher salt

Chop the eggplant and bell peppers into 1/4-inch pieces. Combine the eggplant, bell peppers, onion, garlic, water, lemon juice, brown sugar and 1 teaspoon salt in a saucepan and mix well. Simmer for 15 minutes or until the vegetables are tender and most of the liquid has been absorbed, stirring occasionally. Stir in the raisins and capers. Let stand until room temperature. Stir in the parsley. May be prepared up to 2 days in advance and stored, covered, in the refrigerator.

Crush the anise seeds using a mortar and pestle or an electric coffee or spice grinder. Cut the lavash into thirty-six 1 3/4-inch squares, discarding the trimmings. Soak 12 of the squares in water in a bowl for 15 seconds. Remove the squares. Scrape a thin layer of the bread from each square using the edge of a spoon. Press the squares white side up into 12 miniature muffin cups. Sprinkle with some of the anise seeds and kosher salt. Place the muffin cups on the middle oven rack. Bake at 350 degrees in a preheated oven for 15 minutes or until brown and crisp. Cool in muffin cups on a wire rack. Repeat the process with the remaining lavash, anise seeds and kosher salt. May be prepared up to 2 days in advance and stored in an airtight container at room temperature. Spoon the caponata into the lavash cups just before serving.
Yield: 36 servings.

Clams Casino

25 large quahog clams in shells, cleaned
Tabasco sauce to taste
1 large green bell pepper
1 large onion
1 sleeve butter crackers, crushed
25 slices bacon
1/2 cup (1 stick) butter, melted
1/2 cup lemon juice
Cayenne pepper to taste

Separate the clams into halves, leaving the clams on 1 of the shells and discarding the other half of each shell. Place a dash of Tabasco sauce under each clam. Place the clams on a baking sheet.

Process the green pepper and onion in a food processor until chopped. Combine the green pepper mixture and cracker crumbs in a bowl and mix well. Spread 1 tablespoon of the crumb mixture over each clam. Drape 1 bacon slice over each clam.

Broil in a preheated oven until the bacon is cooked through and the clams are heated through. Brush with a mixture of the butter, lemon juice and cayenne pepper. Arrange on a serving platter. Yield: 25 servings.

Ancient Athenians are credited with inventing the hors d'oeuvres trolley. According to Lynceus, a dinner featuring samplings of items like garlic, wine sop, sea urchins, and cockles, was an insult to a hungry man, "for the cook sets before you a large tray on which there are five small plates....While I am eating this, another is eating that; and while he is eating that, I have made away with this. What I want, good sir, is both the one and the other, but my wish is impossible....Such a layout as that," he concluded, "may seem to offer variety, but is nothing at all to satisfy the belly."

Stuffed Quahogs

25 quahog clams
1/2 (12-ounce) can beer
32 ounces bulk sausage
1 large Vidalia onion
1 red bell pepper
1 green bell pepper
1 yellow bell pepper
1 cup shredded cheese
1 (12-ounce) package butter crackers, crushed

Place the clams in a 5-quart bowl or pan. Pour the beer over the clams. Add just enough water to cover the clams. Remove the clams from the beer mixture when they open. Remove the clam meat, reserving the broth. Clean the shells.

Brown the sausage in a skillet, stirring until crumbly; drain. Process the onion, red pepper, green pepper and yellow pepper in a food processor until minced. Add the clams and cheese. Process until mixed. Stir in the sausage. Add the cracker crumbs and mix well. Add the reserved broth until of a paste consistency and mix well.

Spoon the clam mixture into the clam shells. Arrange the shells on a baking sheet. Bake at 350 degrees in a preheated oven for 10 to 15 minutes or until golden brown. Serve warm. May freeze the baked clams for future use. Yield: 25 to 30 servings.

Savory Summer Clams on the Half-Shell

1 cup (2 sticks) unsalted butter, softened
3/4 cup butter cracker crumbs
1/2 cup chopped fresh herbs (parsley, chives, oregano, thyme or other seasonal herbs)
1 egg yolk, beaten
2 to 3 garlic cloves, crushed or minced
1/2 teaspoon Tabasco sauce
Rock salt
48 rinsed freshly shucked littleneck clams on the half-shell

Combine the butter, cracker crumbs, herbs, egg yolk, garlic and Tabasco sauce in a bowl and mix well. Shape into a 12-inch log on plastic wrap. Chill, covered with plastic wrap, until firm. May be prepared several days in advance and stored, covered, in the refrigerator or frozen for up to 1 week.

Spread the rock salt on a baking sheet with sides. Arrange the clams on the salt to keep the shells steady. Top each clam with an 1/8-inch-thick slice of the herb butter. Broil 8 inches from the heat source in a preheated oven for 10 minutes or until golden brown and bubbly, rotating the baking sheet as needed for even cooking. Transfer the clams to a serving platter. Garnish with sprigs of fresh parsley and lemon wedges. Serve immediately.
Yield: 48 clams.

Although the All-American Soap Box Derby began in Dayton, Ohio, it really picked up speed after moving to Akron in its second year. The races are held at Akron's Derby Downs, and kids across the country and around the world continue to build their own rolling race cars in hopes of earning fame and scholarships by winning the world championship there.

Crab Tartlets

2 (6 ounces each) packages frozen snow crab meat, thawed
1/2 red bell pepper, finely chopped
1/2 green bell pepper, finely chopped
1 rib celery, finely chopped
1/2 cup mayonnaise
Chopped fresh dillweed to taste
Salt and pepper to taste
60 tartlet shells

Combine the crab meat, red pepper, green pepper and celery in a bowl and mix gently. Stir in the mayonnaise. Add the dillweed, salt and pepper and mix well. Chill, covered, in the refrigerator.

Bake the shells using package directions. Let stand until cool. Spoon the chilled crab meat mixture into the shells. Garnish with sprigs of fresh dillweed. Serve immediately or chill, covered, until serving time. Yield: 60 tartlets.

Spicy Crab Claws

3 pounds cooked crab claws
1 cup minced scallions
½ cup chopped fresh parsley
2 ribs celery, chopped
3 garlic cloves, crushed
1 cup olive oil
½ cup tarragon vinegar
3 tablespoons lemon juice
1 tablespoon Worcestershire sauce
⅛ teaspoon Tabasco sauce
Salt and freshly ground pepper to taste
Butter to taste
Black bread, sliced

Clean the claws with a vegetable scrub brush. Arrange the claws in a bowl. Combine the scallions, parsley, celery and garlic in a saucepan and mix well. Stir in the olive oil, tarragon vinegar, lemon juice, Worcestershire sauce, Tabasco sauce, salt and pepper.

Cook just until heated through, stirring occasionally. Pour over the claws, turning to coat. Marinate, covered, in the refrigerator for 8 to 10 hours. Let stand at room temperature for 1 hour before serving. Drain ⅔ of the marinade before serving. Serve with buttered black bread. Yield: 24 servings.

The ancient Romans kept snails, fed them herbs, and feasted on them all year round—ancient escargot!

Crab and Portobello Appetizers

6 medium portobello mushrooms
2 tablespoons olive oil
1 small jar roasted red bell peppers, drained
1 teaspoon rosemary
1/2 teaspoon salt
Freshly ground pepper
4 ounces crab meat
3 ounces bleu cheese, crumbled

Remove the stems from the mushrooms and discard. Place the mushrooms in a sealable plastic bag. Drizzle with the olive oil and seal tightly. Let stand for 30 minutes, turning the bag frequently. Grill the mushrooms over hot coals for 10 minutes or broil in a preheated oven for 5 minutes.

Arrange the mushrooms in a single layer on a baking sheet. Top with the red peppers. Sprinkle with the rosemary, salt and pepper. Top with the crab meat and sprinkle with the cheese. Bake at 350 degrees in a preheated oven for 2 to 3 minutes or until bubbly. Garnish with sprigs of fresh parsley. Yield: 6 servings.

Broiled Goat Cheese

Goat cheese with rind, cut into 1/2-inch slices, frozen
Honey to taste
Thyme to taste
Assorted party crackers

Arrange the cheese slices in a single layer in an ovenproof dish sprayed with nonstick cooking spray. Broil in a preheated oven until brown on top. Drizzle with honey and sprinkle with thyme. Serve with assorted party crackers. Yield: variable.

Goat Cheese and Eggplant Wraps

4 or 5 medium oriental eggplant
Salt and freshly ground pepper to taste
5 tablespoons olive oil
6 ounces goat cheese
1/4 cup finely chopped Greek olives
1/2 cup flour
2 eggs, lightly beaten
1 1/2 cups fresh bread crumbs
6 cups vegetable oil

Trim the ends from the eggplant. Cut the eggplant lengthwise into twenty-four 1/4-inch slices. Sprinkle lightly with salt and pepper. Heat 2 tablespoons of the olive oil in a large nonstick skillet over medium-high heat. Cook the eggplant in batches in a single layer in the hot olive oil for 2 to 4 minutes per side or until tender and golden brown; drain. Repeat the process with the remaining olive oil and remaining eggplant slices.

Combine the goat cheese and olives in a bowl and mix well. Spoon 1 heaping teaspoon of the cheese mixture in the center of each eggplant strip. Wrap the eggplant around the cheese mixture to enclose. Coat the wraps with the flour, shaking off the excess. Dip in the egg and coat with the bread crumbs.

Pour just enough of the vegetable oil into a heavy saucepan to measure 3 inches. Heat to 375 degrees. Fry the wraps in batches for 30 seconds or until golden brown on all sides; drain. Serve immediately. The wraps may be prepared 1 day in advance and stored, covered, in the refrigerator. Reheat wraps on a baking sheet at 375 degrees in a preheated oven for 10 minutes. May substitute a larger eggplant for the oriental eggplant, slicing into 2x7-inch strips. Yield: 24 wraps.

Garlic, a bulbous vegetable, is actually a member of the lily family, which also includes onions, shallots, leeks, and scallions. Stored in a cool, dry place, garlic will keep for up to one month.

Miniature Lamb Kabobs

1/4 cup red wine vinegar
1 tablespoon soy sauce
1 tablespoon dry sherry
1/2 teaspoon dried rosemary
1/2 teaspoon dried thyme
2 garlic cloves, lightly crushed
1 1/2 pounds lamb, cut into 1/2-inch cubes
Cherry tomatoes
Green bell peppers, cut into 1-inch chunks
Small white onions
Mushrooms

Whisk the wine vinegar, soy sauce, sherry, rosemary, thyme and
garlic in a bowl. Add the lamb, tossing to coat. Marinate, covered,
in the refrigerator for 8 to 10 hours, stirring occasionally. Drain,
reserving the marinade.

Thread the lamb alternately with 2 cherry tomatoes, 1 green
pepper chunk and 1 onion on each skewer. Arrange the skewers
on a broiler rack in a broiler pan. Broil in a preheated oven for
10 minutes or until the lamb is done to taste, basting frequently
with the reserved marinade. Serve immediately. Yield: 6 servings.

Mushroom Cups

12 ounces mushrooms, chopped
3 tablespoons butter or margarine
8 ounces cream cheese, softened
2 egg yolks, lightly beaten
1 1/2 teaspoons salt
1 1/4 teaspoons minced garlic
Cracked pepper to taste
45 phyllo pastry cups

Sauté the mushrooms in the butter in a skillet until tender. Remove from heat. Stir in the cream cheese, egg yolks, salt, garlic and pepper. Spoon the mushroom mixture into the pastry cups. Arrange on a baking sheet. Bake at 350 degrees in a preheated oven for 15 minutes. Serve warm or at room temperature. Yield: 45 servings.

Crab-Stuffed Mushrooms

6 ounces frozen crab meat, thawed, drained
1/3 cup mayonnaise
2 tablespoons each minced celery and minced onion
2 tablespoons bread crumbs
1 tablespoon lemon juice
1 tablespoon dry sherry
1/4 teaspoon salt
1/8 teaspoon hot pepper sauce
12 medium mushroom caps
2 tablespoons vegetable oil

Combine the crab meat, mayonnaise, celery, onion, bread crumbs, lemon juice, sherry, salt and pepper sauce in a bowl and mix well. Brush the mushroom caps lightly with the oil. Spoon some of the crab meat mixture into each cap. Arrange the mushrooms in a single layer on a baking sheet lined with waxed paper. Freeze until firm. Arrange the mushrooms on a baking sheet. Bake at 400 degrees in a preheated oven for 10 minutes or until heated through. Serve immediately. May be placed in a freezer container and stored in the freezer. Yield: 12 servings.

Lead singer and founding member of the rock group The Pretenders, Chrissie Hynde traces her beginnings back to Akron, where she grew up. This legendary artist remains close to friends and family who still live in the area.

Curried Mushroom Turnovers

3 1/2 cups minced fresh mushrooms
3/4 cup minced shallots
2 tablespoons flour
1/2 teaspoon curry powder
1/2 teaspoon salt
1/4 teaspoon cumin
1/4 teaspoon pepper
1/2 cup plain reduced-fat yogurt
2 tablespoons chopped fresh cilantro
14 sheets frozen phyllo pastry, thawed

Spray a large nonstick skillet with butter-flavor nonstick cooking spray. Heat over medium-high heat. Add the mushrooms and shallots to the skillet. Cook for 11 minutes or until all of the moisture has been absorbed, stirring constantly. Stir in a mixture of the flour, curry powder, salt, cumin and pepper. Cook for 3 minutes or until thickened, stirring constantly. Remove from heat. Stir in the yogurt and cilantro.

Unroll the phyllo pastry and cover it with waxed paper topped with a damp towel. Keep the unused portion covered until needed to prevent drying out. Remove 1 sheet of the pastry. Cut lengthwise into halves. Coat the halves lightly with butter-flavor nonstick cooking spray. Fold the halves lengthwise into halves to form strips.

Spoon 1 tablespoon of the mushroom mixture in the corner of each strip. Fold the corner over to the opposite edge to form a triangle. Continue folding as for a flag. Arrange the triangle seam side down on a baking sheet. Spray lightly with butter-flavor nonstick cooking spray. Repeat the process with the remaining pastry and mushroom mixture. Bake at 400 degrees in a preheated oven for 15 minutes or until golden brown. Serve immediately.
Yield: 28 turnovers.

Mushroom Turnovers

1 1/2 cups flour
8 ounces cream cheese, softened
1/2 cup (1 stick) butter or margarine, softened
8 ounces mushrooms, chopped
1 large onion, chopped
3 tablespoons butter or margarine
1/4 cup sour cream
2 tablespoons flour
1 teaspoon salt
1/4 teaspoon thyme
1 egg, beaten

Combine 1 1/2 cups flour, cream cheese and 1/2 cup butter in a mixing bowl. Beat at medium speed until blended, scraping the bowl occasionally. Shape the dough into a ball. Chill, wrapped in plastic wrap, for 1 hour.

Sauté the mushrooms and onion in 3 tablespoons butter in a 10-inch skillet until tender. Stir in the sour cream, 2 tablespoons flour, salt and thyme. Remove from heat.

Divide the dough into 2 portions. Roll 1 portion 1/8 inch thick on a lightly floured surface. Cut into rounds with a floured 2 3/4-inch cutter. Repeat the process with the remaining dough.

Spoon 1 teaspoon of the cream cheese mixture on half of each round. Brush the edges of the rounds with some of the egg. Fold over to enclose the filling. Press the edges with a fork to seal; prick the tops. Arrange the turnovers on an ungreased baking sheet. Brush with the remaining egg. Bake at 450 degrees in a preheated oven for 12 to 14 minutes or until golden brown. Yield: 42 turnovers.

"Prosciutto" is the Italian word for ham. In Italy, certain pigs are bred specifically for prosciutto production. These pigs are fed the whey that is left over from making Parmesan cheese, which gives their meat its delicate flavor.

Palmiers with Prosciutto

1 (11x18-inch) sheet puff pastry
3 tablespoons honey mustard
4 ounces thinly sliced prosciutto
3/4 cup freshly grated Parmesan cheese
1 egg
2 teaspoons water

Place the puff pastry on a hard surface. Spread with the honey mustard. Arrange the prosciutto over the mustard. Sprinkle with the cheese. Press the cheese lightly into the prosciutto with a rolling pin. Starting at 1 long end, roll as for a jelly roll just to the middle of the pastry. Roll the other side to make 2 rolls that meet in the center. Cut down the center using a serrated knife. Cut each roll into 1/2-inch slices.

Arrange the slices cut side up on a baking sheet lined with parchment paper. Press lightly to flatten. Chill for 15 minutes. Whisk the egg and water in a bowl. Brush the top of each with the egg wash. Bake at 400 degrees in a preheated oven for 10 minutes or until puffed and golden brown. Serve warm or at room temperature.

For variety, spread the puff pastry with 1/3 cup pesto and sprinkle with 1 cup grated Parmesan cheese for variety. Press the cheese into the dough using a rolling pin and proceed with above directions. Yield: 20 palmiers.

Bacon-Wrapped Oysters à la Teddy Roosevelt

60 oysters
15 slices bacon, cut into fourths

Wrap the oysters in the bacon and secure with wooden picks. Arrange the wrapped oysters in a single layer on a broiler rack in a broiler pan. Broil in a preheated oven until the bacon is crisp and the edges of the oysters curl. Yield: 60 servings.

Pinehurst Pecans

1 1/2 pounds pecan halves
2 tablespoons coarsely chopped fresh rosemary
3/4 teaspoon cayenne pepper
1 tablespoon sugar
1 tablespoon kosher salt
2 tablespoons unsalted butter, melted

Spread the pecans in a single layer on a baking sheet. Toast at 350 degrees in a preheated oven for 10 minutes or until golden brown, stirring occasionally.

Combine the rosemary, cayenne pepper, sugar and kosher salt in a bowl and mix well. Stir in the butter. Add the warm pecans and toss to coat. May be prepared in advance and stored in airtight tins. Note: Do not use dried rosemary in this recipe.
Yield: 12 servings.

The oyster is "in itself a simple service of exquisite quality, brought to the table with the attendant graces of mild and delicate vinegar or lemon juice, brown bread and butter, and a glass of light Chablis for those who take it; the half-dozen natives occupying the hollow shells, bathed in their own liquor, hold rank of a very different kind to that of the miscellaneous assortment of tidbits which are usually demanded by foreign gastronomic taste."

—from Good Cheer: The Romance of Food and Feasting

Potato Cakes with Portobellos

2¹/₂ pounds russet potatoes (about 6 potatoes)
Salt to taste
1¹/₂ teaspoons marjoram, crushed
1¹/₂ teaspoons tarragon, crushed
1¹/₂ teaspoons basil, crushed
4 to 5 ounces portobello mushrooms, thickly sliced
3 tablespoons olive oil
Pepper to taste
¹/₂ cup sliced shallots
¹/₂ cup sliced leek bulb
¹/₄ cup (¹/₂ stick) butter
5 ounces prosciutto, thinly sliced, chopped
1¹/₂ cups shredded Emmentaler or Gruyère cheese

Combine the potatoes and salt with enough water to cover in a saucepan. Bring to a boil. Boil for 30 minutes or until tender; drain. Cool for 15 minutes. Peel the potatoes. Mash the potatoes in a bowl. Stir in the marjoram, tarragon and basil.

Brush the mushrooms with 2 tablespoons of the olive oil. Season with salt and pepper. Arrange on a broiler rack in a broiler pan. Broil in a preheated oven for 5 to 8 minutes or until tender. Chop coarsely.

Heat the remaining 1 tablespoon olive oil in a skillet over high heat. Add the shallots and leek. Sauté until tender. Stir in the potato mixture. Add the mushrooms and stir gently. Shape the mushroom mixture by ¹/₂ cupfuls into 3- to 4-inch cakes.

Heat 2 tablespoons of the butter in a large skillet over medium-high heat until melted. Add the cakes in batches. Cook for 4 minutes per side or until golden brown, adding the remaining 2 tablespoons butter as needed. Remove the cakes with a slotted spoon to a lightly oiled baking sheet. Top each cake with prosciutto and sprinkle with cheese. Bake at 400 degrees in a preheated oven for 10 minutes or until the cheese melts. Arrange on a serving platter or on individual plates. Garnish with sprigs of fresh parsley or basil. Serve immediately. May prepare the cakes in advance up to the baking step and store, covered, in the refrigerator. Bake just before serving. Yield: 10 to 12 cakes.

Red Potatoes with Caviar

12 small red potatoes
Salt and pepper to taste
1/2 cup crème fraîche
1 ounce golden caviar

Combine the potatoes with enough water to cover in a saucepan. Bring to a boil. Boil for 10 to 15 minutes or until tender; drain. Let stand until cool. Cut the potatoes into halves. Scoop the pulp from the middle of each potato half with a small spoon or a melon baller, leaving a shell. Season the cavities with salt and pepper.

Spoon the crème fraîche into the potato cavities. Top each half with some of the caviar. Arrange on a serving platter.
Yield: 24 servings.

Bacon-Wrapped Scallops

Bay or sea scallops
Teriyaki sauce
Bacon slices, cut into halves

Rinse and drain the scallops. Cut the large scallops into halves. Place in a bowl. Pour teriyaki sauce over the scallops and toss to coat. Marinate, covered, in the refrigerator for a few hours or up to overnight, stirring occasionally; drain.

Wrap each scallop with a bacon half and secure with a wooden pick. Arrange on a baking sheet with sides. Drizzle with teriyaki sauce. Bake at 425 degrees in a preheated oven until the bacon is crisp, turning once. Yield: variable.

Established in 1936, Akron's West Point Market is among the premier gourmet food markets in the nation.

Crispy Dipping Shrimp

1 1/2 cups heavy cream
1 1/2 teaspoons frozen orange juice concentrate
1 teaspoon prepared horseradish
1 teaspoon prepared mustard
Salt and pepper to taste
12 medium shrimp, peeled, deveined
1/2 cup flour
1 egg, lightly beaten
1 (1-pound) package shredded phyllo pastry (see Note)
Vegetable oil for deep-frying

Heat the heavy cream in a saucepan until reduced by half, stirring frequently. Stir in the orange juice concentrate, horseradish and mustard. Season with salt and pepper. Set aside.

Coat the shrimp with the flour and dip in the egg. Wrap the shrimp completely with the phyllo pastry. Thread 2 shrimp on each of 6 bamboo skewers. Pour enough oil into a skillet to measure 1 to 2 inches. Heat to 375 degrees. Fry the shrimp skewers in the hot oil for 3 to 5 minutes or until golden brown; drain. Serve with the sauce. Note: If shredded pastry is not available, cut phyllo into thin strips. Yield: 6 servings.

Marinated Shrimp

1 pound jumbo shrimp, cooked
1/2 cup olive oil
1/2 cup vegetable oil
2 tablespoons tarragon vinegar
Juice of 1/2 lemon
3 tablespoons chopped fresh oregano
1 1/2 teaspoons kosher salt

Peel and devein the shrimp, leaving the tails intact. Whisk the olive oil, vegetable oil, tarragon vinegar and lemon juice in a bowl. Stir in the oregano and kosher salt. Add the shrimp, tossing to coat. Marinate, covered, in the refrigerator for 3 to 4 hours, stirring occasionally; drain. Spoon the shrimp into a serving bowl. Garnish with sprigs of fresh parsley. Yield: 12 servings.

Shrimp Wrapped with Snow Peas

1 pound large shrimp (about 30 shrimp), peeled, deveined
1 bay leaf
1/2 cup extra-virgin olive oil
3 tablespoons white wine vinegar
3 tablespoons Dijon mustard
1 tablespoon chopped fresh dillweed
1 tablespoon chopped shallots
1 teaspoon finely minced gingerroot
1 garlic clove, finely minced
1/8 teaspoon sugar
Salt and pepper to taste
20 snow peas, trimmed

Bring a large stockpot of water to a boil. Add the shrimp and bay leaf. Boil for 2 to 3 minutes or until the shrimp turn pink; drain. Plunge the shrimp into cold water in a bowl to stop the cooking process; drain.

Combine the olive oil, vinegar, Dijon mustard, dillweed, shallots, gingerroot, garlic, sugar, salt and pepper in a jar with a tight-fitting lid. Shake to mix. Pour over the shrimp in a bowl and toss to coat. Marinate, covered, in the refrigerator for 24 hours, stirring once or twice.

Blanch the snow peas in boiling water in a saucepan for 30 seconds; drain. Plunge the snow peas into cold water in a bowl; drain. Separate the snow peas into halves. Wrap each shrimp with a snow pea half and secure with a wooden pick. Serve chilled or at room temperature. Yield: 30 servings.

"The beginning of knowledge is the discovery of something we do not understand."

—*Frank Herbert*

Spicy Cajun Shrimp

½ cup (1 stick) unsalted butter
1 (4-ounce) can minced clams
¼ cup beer, at room temperature
3 garlic cloves, minced
1 tablespoon red pepper flakes
1 teaspoon thyme
1 teaspoon rosemary
1 teaspoon oregano
1 teaspoon basil
1 teaspoon Cajun pepper
1 teaspoon Worcestershire sauce
1 pound shrimp, peeled, deveined, cooked
1 loaf French bread, sliced

Heat the butter in a saucepan until melted. Add the undrained clams, beer, garlic, red pepper flakes, thyme, rosemary, oregano, basil, Cajun pepper and Worcestershire sauce and mix well. Add the shrimp and mix well.

Sauté over medium heat until heated through. Spoon into a serving bowl. Serve warm with seafood forks or fancy wooden picks. Surround the shrimp with the French bread. May also spoon over hot cooked pasta. Yield: 8 servings.

Fabulous Fin and Feather Sampler

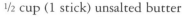

Professional golf has strong ties to the Akron area. The PGA Championship began in 1960, the American Golf Classic in 1961, and the World Series of Golf in 1962—all at Firestone Country Club.

¹/₂ cup (1 stick) unsalted butter
1 teaspoon paprika
1 teaspoon cayenne pepper
1 teaspoon oregano
1 teaspoon thyme
1 teaspoon salt
1 teaspoon onion powder
1 teaspoon black pepper
1 teaspoon garlic powder
2 boneless skinless chicken breasts, cubed
1 or 2 swordfish steaks, cubed
Creole Dipping Sauce

Heat the butter in a saucepan until melted. Stir in the paprika, cayenne pepper, oregano, thyme, salt, onion powder, black pepper and garlic powder. Add the chicken and swordfish and toss to coat. Spoon into a shallow baking pan. Broil in a preheated oven for 10 to 12 minutes or until the chicken is cooked through and the fish flakes easily, stirring occasionally. Serve warm with Creole Dipping Sauce, lemon wedges and pita bread.
Yield: 8 to 10 servings.

Creole Dipping Sauce
1 medium onion, chopped
1 medium green bell pepper, chopped
1 garlic clove, crushed
1 tablespoon olive oil
2 cups marinara sauce
¹/₂ cup chopped black olives
¹/₂ cup white wine
¹/₈ teaspoon thyme

Sauté the onion, green pepper and garlic in the olive oil in a saucepan until tender. Stir in the marinara sauce, black olives, white wine and thyme. Simmer over low heat for 1 hour, stirring occasionally. Serve warm or at room temperature. Yield: 2 cups.

Spinach Turnovers

16 ounces cream cheese, softened
3/4 cup (1 1/2 sticks) butter, softened
2 1/2 cups flour
3/4 teaspoon salt
1 (10-ounce) package frozen chopped spinach, thawed, drained
1/2 cup chopped green onions
4 garlic cloves, chopped
1 tablespoon butter
1 1/2 cups (12 ounces) small curd cottage cheese
1/2 teaspoon pepper
2 eggs, beaten
2 tablespoons milk

Beat the cream cheese and 3/4 cup butter in a mixing bowl until blended. Add the flour and salt and mix well. Knead the dough by hand. Shape into a ball. Place in a sealable plastic bag. Chill for 8 to 10 hours.

Squeeze the excess moisture from the spinach. Sauté the green onions and garlic in 1 tablespoon butter in a large skillet until tender. Stir in the spinach, cottage cheese and pepper.

Roll half the dough 1/8-inch thick on a lightly floured surface. Cut into rounds with a 3-inch cutter. Repeat the process with the remaining dough. Place 1 teaspoon of the spinach mixture on half of each round. Whisk the eggs and milk in a bowl until blended. Brush the edges of the circles with the egg mixture. Fold the rounds over to enclose the filling. Press the edges with a fork to seal. Pierce the tops with a fork. Arrange the turnovers on an ungreased baking sheet. Bake at 425 degrees in a preheated oven for 10 minutes or until light brown. Yield: 80 turnovers.

Spinach Cheese Puffs

1 (10-ounce) package frozen chopped spinach, thawed, drained
1 cup milk
1/2 cup (1 stick) butter or margarine
1 teaspoon salt
1 cup flour
4 eggs
1 cup shredded Gruyère or Swiss cheese
1/2 cup grated Parmesan cheese

Squeeze the excess moisture from the spinach with paper towels. Combine the milk, butter and salt in a 3-quart saucepan. Bring to a boil over medium heat, stirring frequently. Boil until the butter melts. Remove from heat. Add the flour all at once, stirring with a wooden spoon until the mixture forms a ball. Add the eggs 1 at a time, mixing until smooth and satiny after each addition. Stir in the spinach, Gruyère cheese and Parmesan cheese. May be stored, covered, in the refrigerator at this point until just before baking.

Drop the batter by level tablespoons 1 1/2 inches apart onto a lightly greased baking sheet. Bake at 375 degrees in a preheated oven for 15 to 20 minutes or until golden brown. Transfer to a serving platter. Serve immediately. Yield: 48 puffs.

The early landowners and founders of the Akron area were principally from Connecticut. Many of the early buildings were patterned after those in the East. For example, the Historic Church on Tallmadge Circle, built in 1822, is almost a mirror image of the church in Litchfield, Connecticut, the home of Benjamin Tallmadge for whom the city is named, and is considered one of the best examples of New England church architecture in the Western Reserve.

Triconas

16 ounces cream cheese, softened
8 ounces feta cheese, crumbled
2 tablespoons butter or margarine, melted
1 egg, lightly beaten
1 (16-ounce) package frozen phyllo pastry, thawed
1 cup butter, melted

Combine the cream cheese, feta cheese, 2 tablespoons butter and egg in a saucepan. Cook just until blended, stirring constantly. Remove from heat.

Unroll the pastry and cover it with waxed paper topped with a damp towel. Keep the unused portion covered until needed to prevent drying out.

Remove 2 sheets of the pastry and arrange on a hard surface. Brush each sheet with some of the melted butter. Cut each sheet lengthwise into strips 2 inches wide. Spoon 1 teaspoon of the cheese mixture at the end of each strip. Fold the corner over to the opposite edge to cover the filling and form a triangle. Continue folding as for a flag.

Arrange the triangle on an ungreased baking sheet. Repeat the process with the remaining pastry, butter and cheese filling. Bake at 350 degrees in a preheated oven for 20 minutes or until golden brown. Serve immediately. May bake the Triconas in advance and chill, covered, until just before serving. Reheat at 350 degrees in a preheated oven for 10 minutes. May be prepared in advance and frozen unbaked if desired. Bake as needed. Yield: 84 servings.

Incredible Won Tons

1/3 pound ground pork
1/3 pound ground veal
1/3 pound ground turkey
1 (8-ounce) can water chestnuts, drained, finely chopped
1/2 cup oyster sauce
1 bunch scallions, finely chopped
1 (14-ounce) package won ton wrappers
2 tablespoons sesame oil
Vegetable oil for frying

Combine the ground pork, ground veal, ground turkey, water chestnuts, oyster sauce and scallions in a bowl and mix well. Spoon 1 teaspoon of the ground pork mixture on each won ton wrapper. Moisten the edges and fold as desired.

Pour the sesame oil and enough vegetable oil into a skillet to measure 1/4 inch. Heat over medium heat until hot. Add the won tons. Fry for 3 minutes per side or until golden brown; drain. Serve immediately. Yield: 40 won tons.

Raspberry Cheese Gift Box

1 sheet frozen puff pastry
8 to 12 ounces Monterey Jack cheese, thinly sliced
1/4 cup raspberry jam
5 tablespoons finely chopped walnuts

Thaw the puff pastry using package directions. Unfold the pastry sheet on a baking sheet and smooth. Place the cheese in the center of the sheet. Spread the jam evenly over the cheese. Sprinkle with 3 tablespoons of the walnuts. Fold the sides of the pastry to the center to cover the filling and pinch the edges to seal. Sprinkle with the remaining 2 tablespoons walnuts. Bake at 350 degrees in a preheated oven for 20 to 25 minutes or until golden brown. Cut into 1-inch slices. Serve warm. Yield: 10 to 12 servings.

Built on such a high elevation, Akron has its share of steep roads and curves. The most infamous is Bates Street (nicknamed "Cadillac Hill" due to is proximity to the local car dealership). Its average grade is 24.7 percent; the grade is 25.5 percent at its steepest point. That's about as steep as San Francisco's famous Lombard Street, which had an average grade of 26 percent before it was regraded in 1923. Still a brick road, which adds to the experience, Cadillac Hill remains one of the roughest adventure rides in the area.

New England Clam Chowder

2 slices bacon, coarsely chopped
1 cup chopped onion
2 cups cubed peeled potatoes
1 cup water
1 teaspoon salt
1/8 teaspoon pepper
1 pint fresh clams
2 cups half-and-half
2 tablespoons butter or margarine
1 teaspoon thyme

Sauté the bacon in a saucepan until almost crisp. Add the onion and mix well. Cook for 5 minutes, stirring frequently. Stir in the potatoes, water, salt and pepper. Cook for 15 minutes or until the potatoes are tender, stirring occasionally.

Drain the clams, reserving 1/2 cup of the liquid. Chop the clams coarsely. Add the reserved liquid, clams and half-and-half to the potato mixture and mix well. Stir in the butter and thyme. Cook for 3 minutes, stirring occasionally; do not boil. Ladle into soup bowls. Yield: 4 servings.

Oyster Stew

1 pint fresh oysters
6 tablespoons (3/4 stick) butter
Salt and pepper to taste
2 cups cream or milk

Drain the oysters, reserving the liquor. Heat the butter in a saucepan until melted. Add the oysters. Simmer for several minutes or until the edges curl. Season with salt and pepper. Stir in the cream. Bring just to the boiling point, stirring occasionally. Add the reserved oyster liquor to taste. Ladle into soup bowls. Serve with oyster crackers. Yield: 4 servings.

Spinach Soup

3 (16 ounces each) cans chicken stock
2 carrots, sliced
2 ribs celery, sliced
2 cups fresh spinach, torn into bite-size pieces
3 tablespoons butter
3 tablespoons flour
2 egg yolks
1 tablespoon lemon juice
2 tablespoons minced fresh parsley
3/4 teaspoon dillweed
1/4 teaspoon salt
1/4 teaspoon pepper

Reserve 1 cup of the stock. Combine the remaining stock, carrots and celery in a saucepan. Cook until the vegetables are tender-crisp, stirring occasionally. Add the spinach and mix well. Simmer for 5 minutes, stirring occasionally.

Heat the butter in a saucepan until melted. Add the flour, stirring until blended. Stir in the reserved stock. Cook until thickened, stirring constantly. Add to the spinach mixture and mix well. Simmer for 15 minutes, stirring occasionally.

Whisk the egg yolks and lemon juice in a bowl until blended. Add 1/2 cup of the hot stock mixture and mix well. Stir into the spinach mixture. Bring just to a boil, stirring occasionally. Stir in the parsley, dillweed, salt and pepper. Ladle into soup bowls. Yield: 4 servings.

Once known as the "Rubber Capital of the World," Akron today is a world-renowned center for polymer research and development. Approximately 400 polymer-related companies are located in the Akron area, and the University of Akron is among the top universities for the study of polymer science.

Tortellini with Smoked Salmon

12 ounces frozen cheese tortellini, cooked, drained
1/4 cup (1/2 stick) butter, softened
1 garlic clove, crushed
1/2 teaspoon each chopped fresh parsley and salt
1/3 teaspoon finely chopped fresh dillweed
1/4 teaspoon basil
6 ounces white American cheese, shredded
1/2 cup heavy cream
4 ounces smoked salmon, chopped
2 tablespoons coarsely grated Parmesan cheese

Mix the cooked tortellini, butter, garlic, parsley, salt, dillweed and basil in a bowl. Pour the heavy cream into a microwave-safe dish. Microwave on High for 1 minute; stir. Microwave for 30 seconds or until warm. Add to the tortellini mixture; mix well. Stir in the salmon. Spoon the tortellini onto 4 to 6 plates. Sprinkle with the cheese. Garnish with sprigs of fresh parsley. Serve immediately. Yield: 4 to 6 servings.

Auntie's Antipasti

1 (14-ounce) can artichoke hearts, drained, chopped
1 small jar roasted red bell peppers, drained, thinly sliced
8 ounces Swedish fontina cheese, cubed
4 ounces prosciutto, shredded
1/2 (8-ounce) can black olives, drained, sliced
1 tablespoon chopped fresh parsley
2 garlic cloves, minced
1/4 cup olive oil
French bread baguettes, sliced

Combine the artichokes, roasted red peppers, cheese, prosciutto, black olives, parsley and garlic in a bowl and mix gently. Add the olive oil and toss to coat.

Chill, covered, for 1 hour or longer before serving. Serve with sliced French bread. Yield: 6 to 8 servings.

Bocconcini

Small fresh mozzarella balls
4 ounces roasted red bell peppers
Roma tomatoes, sliced
1 (6-ounce) jar marinated artichoke hearts
Salt and freshly ground pepper to taste
Extra-virgin olive oil to taste

Slice 1 mozzarella ball per guest. Arrange cheese, roasted red peppers, several tomato slices and 2 to 3 artichoke hearts per guest on individual plates. Sprinkle tomato slices with salt and freshly ground pepper if desired. Drizzle with olive oil.
Yield: variable.

Champagne Salad

8 ounces cream cheese, softened
3/4 cup sugar
1 (15-ounce) can pineapple tidbits, drained
3 bananas, sliced
1 (10-ounce) package frozen sliced strawberries, thawed
16 ounces whipped topping

Beat the cream cheese and sugar in a mixing bowl until creamy. Stir in the pineapple, bananas and undrained strawberries gently. Fold in the whipped topping. Chill, covered, for 8 to 10 hours.
Yield: 10 to 12 servings.

Stan Hywet Hall, built by rubber baron Frank A. Seiberling (founder of both Goodyear Tire and Rubber and Seiberling Rubber), is recognized as one of "America's Castles." The 65-room manor house, now a museum, is one of the finest examples of Tudor Revival architecture in the United States. Furnished with priceless antiques and works of art, this breathtaking home is situated on seventy acres of tailored lawns, gardens, woods, and lagoons.

Cucumber Salad

4 cucumbers
Salt to taste
2 tablespoons sugar
2 tablespoons vinegar
2 tablespoons (heaping) sour cream

Cut the cucumbers into paper-thin slices. Layer the cucumbers in a bowl, sprinkling each layer with salt. Chill, covered, for 2 to 10 hours; preferably 10 hours. Rinse the cucumbers and press gently to remove excess moisture. Pat with paper towels.

Combine the sugar, vinegar and sour cream in a bowl and mix well. Add the cucumbers and toss to coat. Yield: 12 to 15 servings.

Frozen Fruit Salad

1/2 cup sugar
1 (8-ounce) can crushed pineapple, drained
2 cups sour cream
2 bananas, chopped
2 tablespoons lemon juice
4 drops of red food coloring
1 (16-ounce) can fruit cocktail, drained

Combine the sugar, pineapple, sour cream, bananas, lemon juice and food coloring in a bowl and mix gently. Fold in the fruit cocktail. Spoon into 12 muffin cups. Cover with plastic wrap; cover with foil. Freeze for 8 to 10 hours. Let stand at room temperature for 30 minutes before serving. Invert onto individual salad plates or onto a serving platter. Yield: 12 servings.

Goat Cheese in Bacon

2 (11 to 12 ounces each) logs goat cheese, cut into 1/2-inch slices
12 slices bacon, cut into halves
2 tablespoons olive oil
1 tablespoon honey
1 tablespoon red wine, balsamic or flavored vinegar
Salt and pepper to taste
8 to 10 ounces mixed greens
2 tomatoes, chopped
1 red onion, sliced
1/2 cup pine nuts, toasted

Wrap the cheese slices in plastic wrap. Freeze until firm. Remove plastic wrap. Wrap each cheese slice in a bacon half. Arrange the slices seam side down in a skillet coated with nonstick cooking spray. Cook over medium heat until the bacon is crisp and cooked through, turning once. Drain on a baking sheet lined with paper towels.

Whisk the olive oil, honey and wine vinegar in a bowl until blended. Season with salt and pepper. Drizzle over the mixed greens in a bowl and toss to coat.

Divide the mixed greens evenly among 12 plates. Sprinkle with the tomatoes, onion and pine nuts. Top each with 2 goat cheese rounds. Yield: 12 servings.

"Every contrivance of man—every tool, every instrument, every utensil, every article designed for use, of each and every kind—evolved from a very simple beginning."

—Robert Collier

Tabouli

1 cup fine grain cracked wheat
2 bunches green onions, finely chopped, or to taste
1½ large bunches parsley, finely chopped, or to taste
⅔ cup finely chopped fresh mint leaves, or ½ cup dried mint
8 to 10 tomatoes, chopped
Juice of 4 lemons, or to taste
¼ cup olive oil
1 teaspoon salt, or to taste
½ teaspoon pepper

Rinse the wheat with water until the water is no longer cloudy.
Soak in warm water to cover in a bowl for 10 minutes; drain.
Squeeze dry by cupping hands and pressing the wheat between the
palms. Combine the wheat, green onions, parsley and mint in a
bowl and mix well. Chill, covered, in the refrigerator. Stir in the
tomatoes. Add the lemon juice, olive oil, salt and pepper and mix
gently. Serve with fresh grape leaves or lettuce leaves to use as
scoops. Yield: 6 servings.

Avocado Boats

1 large ripe avocado, cut into halves
Lemon juice
1 (6-ounce) can crab meat or shrimp, drained
1 small onion, minced
2 tablespoons mayonnaise
1 tablespoon Thousand Island salad dressing
Salt to taste
Pepper to taste
Parsley flakes to taste

Drizzle the avocado halves with lemon juice. Arrange each half
on a salad plate. Combine the crab meat, onion, mayonnaise, salad
dressing and salt in a bowl and mix well. Mound the crab meat
mixture in the avocado halves. Sprinkle with pepper and parsley
flakes. Yield: 2 servings.

Valley Crab Cakes

6 tablespoons (3/4 stick) butter
1/2 cup chopped fresh mushrooms
1/3 cup minced onion
1/3 cup minced green and red bell pepper
1/2 cup heavy cream
2 teaspoons Creole mustard
2 teaspoons Worcestershire sauce
1/2 teaspoon salt
1/2 teaspoon garlic powder
1/2 teaspoon black pepper
1/4 teaspoon white pepper
1/8 teaspoon cayenne pepper
1 cup dry plain bread crumbs
1 pound lump crab meat
2 eggs, lightly beaten
1 cup milk
1 egg
1 1/2 cups flour
Vegetable oil for frying
Creole Mustard Sauce (page 177)

Heat the butter in a skillet until melted. Add the mushrooms, onion and bell pepper. Sauté until tender. Stir in the heavy cream, Creole mustard, Worcestershire sauce, salt, garlic powder, black pepper, white pepper and cayenne pepper. Simmer for 3 minutes, stirring frequently. Remove from heat. Stir in the bread crumbs, crab meat and 2 eggs. Spoon into a bowl. Chill, covered, in the refrigerator. Shape the chilled crab meat mixture into balls about the size of ping pong balls. Pat the balls into cakes. Whisk the milk and 1 egg in a bowl until blended. Dip the cakes into the egg mixture and coat with the flour. Sauté in the hot oil in a skillet until brown on both sides; drain. Serve warm with the Creole Mustard Sauce. Yield: 16 crab cakes.

One of the world's first long-distance electric railways began in Akron: the ABC line—Akron, Bedford, Cleveland.

Creole Mustard Sauce

1 cup sour cream
1 cup heavy cream
¼ cup Creole or whole grain mustard
2½ teaspoons Worcestershire sauce
½ teaspoon each cayenne pepper and garlic powder
¼ teaspoon ground black pepper

Combine the sour cream, heavy cream, Creole mustard,
Worcestershire sauce, cayenne pepper, garlic powder and black
pepper in a saucepan and mix well. Cook until heated through,
stirring frequently. Serve warm. Yield: 2 cups.

Crab Cakes

2 ripe avocados, puréed
2 tablespoons lime juice
1 garlic clove, minced
1 pound fresh or canned crab meat
1 cup bread crumbs
¼ cup chopped fresh parsley
¼ cup mayonnaise
2 eggs, lightly beaten
3 tablespoons chopped green onions
2 tablespoons Dijon mustard
1 tablespoon lime juice
1 teaspoon chopped jalapeño chile
¼ cup (½ stick) butter

Combine the avocado purée, 2 tablespoons lime juice and garlic
in a bowl and mix well. Set aside. Combine the crab meat, bread
crumbs, parsley, mayonnaise, eggs, green onions, Dijon mustard,
1 tablespoon lime juice and jalapeño chile in a bowl and mix
well. Shape into 16 cakes. Heat the butter in a large skillet over
medium heat until melted. Fry the crab cakes in batches until
golden brown on both sides, turning once; drain. Transfer to a
serving platter. Garnish with lime slices and sprigs of fresh parsley.
Serve with the avocado purée. The crab cakes may be prepared in
advance and stored, covered, in the refrigerator. Reheat in the
microwave or oven just until warm. Yield: 16 crab cakes.

Spring Tart with Asparagus and Red Onions

1 recipe Yeast Tart Dough (page 179)
Unbleached flour
2 ounces Gruyère cheese, shredded
1 tablespoon light olive oil
1/2 red onion, thinly sliced
1/4 teaspoon salt
White pepper to taste
8 ounces asparagus, cut diagonally into 1-inch pieces
1/4 teaspoon salt
1 tablespoon chopped fresh chervil or Italian parsley
Salt to taste
3 eggs
1 1/2 cups half-and-half
Minced zest of 1 orange
1/4 teaspoon (heaping) salt

Press the dough in a thin layer over the bottom of a 9-inch tart pan with removable bottom, sprinkling with flour as needed to prevent sticking. Pat the dough in a thicker layer up the side of the pan 1/4 inch above the rim. Sprinkle the cheese over the bottom. Heat the olive oil in a sauté pan until hot. Add the onion, 1/4 teaspoon salt and white pepper. Sauté over medium heat for 7 to 8 minutes or until the onion is tender. Add the asparagus, 1/4 teaspoon salt and white pepper. Cook for 7 to 8 minutes or until the asparagus is tender. Transfer the asparagus mixture to a bowl. Stir in the chervil. Season with salt to taste and white pepper. Let stand until cool. Whisk the eggs in a bowl until blended. Stir in the half-and-half, orange zest and 1/4 heaping teaspoon salt and white pepper. Spoon the asparagus mixture into the prepared pan. Pour the egg mixture over the top. Bake at 375 degrees in a preheated oven for 40 minutes or until golden brown and set. May substitute 1 commercially prepared pie shell for the tart dough. Yield: 16 servings.

Yeast Tart Dough

1 teaspoon dry yeast
1/8 teaspoon sugar
1/4 cup warm (110-degree) water
1 cup (about) unbleached flour
1/2 teaspoon salt
1/2 teaspoon minced lemon zest (optional)
1 egg, at room temperature
3 tablespoons unsalted butter, softened
Unbleached flour

Dissolve the yeast and sugar in the warm water in a bowl. Let stand in a warm place until foamy. Mix 1 cup flour, salt and lemon zest in a bowl. Make a well in the center of the flour mixture. Add the egg, butter and yeast mixture to the well. Mix with a wooden spoon until a soft dough forms. Sprinkle the dough with additional flour; shape into a ball. Place in a bowl. Let rise, covered with plastic wrap, in a warm place for 45 to 60 minutes or until doubled in bulk. Press the dough over the bottom and up the side of a 9-inch tart pan. If the dough shrinks back when shaping, cover the dough and let rest for 20 minutes. Punch the dough down; let rise again if you are not ready to shape the dough. Yield: 1 (9-inch) tart shell.

Bibliography

Akron Beacon Journal. Various articles.

Charpentier, Henri. *Food & Finesse: The Bride's Bible.* W.B. Conkey Company, 1945.

Cole, M. Shawn. "Cole's Quotables." April 2, 1999. <http://www2.xtdl.com/~scole/>.

Dariaux, Genevieve Antoine. *Entertaining with Elegance.* Garden City, New York: Doubleday & Co., 1965.

"Famous Quotes and Quotations: Best Quotes and Familiar Quotations." Starting Page! 1999. <http://www.startingpage.com/html/quotations.html> (April 2, 1999).

Fordyce, Eleanore. *Dining in America.* Margaret Woodbury Strong Museum. 1987.

Ginaven, Marlene. *Not For Us Alone.* Akron, Ohio. 1985.

Hackwood, Frederick W. *Good Cheer: The Romance of Food and Feasting.* London. 1911.

Heaten, Rose Henniker. *The Perfect Hostess.* New York: E.P. Dutton, 1931.

Horander, Edith, of Austria. *The Recipe Book as a Cultural and Socio-Historical Document.* Edinburgh. 1981.

Knepper, George W. *Akron: City at the Summit.* Akron, Ohio. 1994.

Lubbock, Sir John. *Pleasures of Life.* New York: H.M. Caldwell Co., 1887.

Lukins, Sheila and Julee Rosso. *The New Basics Cookbook.* New York: Workman Publishing, 1979.

—with Chase, Sarah Leah. *The Silver Palate Goodtimes Cookbook.* New York: Workman Publishing, 1984.

—with McLaughlin, Michael. *The Silver Palate Cookbook.* New York: Workman Publishing, 1989.

McGovern, Frances. *Written on the Hills: The Making of the Akron Landscape.* Akron, Ohio. 1996.

"Quote Search." *Quotation Collection.* Starlingtech. April 2, 1999 <http://www.starlingtech.com/quotes/index.html>.

Spanoudis, Stephen L. "Quotations." *The Other Pages.* 1994. April 2, 1999 <http://www2.xtdl.com/~scole/>.

Spencer, Colin, and Claire Clifton, ed. *The Faber Book of Food.* Faber and Faber Ltd. 1993.

Stewart, Donald Ogden. *Perfect Behavior.* New York: George H. Doran and Co., 1922.

Summit County Historical Society. Various literature.

Tennyson, Jeffrey. *Hamburger Heaven.* Hyperion. 1993.

"Words of Women: Quotations for Success." *FOD Women In Business Webring.* Power Dynamics. April 2, 1999. <http://www.wordsofwomen.com/cgibin/var/women/index.html>.

Index

BEGINNINGS

A Collection of Appetizers Presented by the

Junior League of Akron
929 West Market Street • Akron, Ohio 44313

(330) 836-4905

Please send _____ copies of *Beginnings* . . . . $22.95 each $ _____

Postage and handling . . . . . . $4.00 first book/$2.00 each additional book $ _____

Ohio residents add 5.75% sales tax (or current tax rate) $ _____

Total $ _____

Name _____

Address _____

City _____ State _____ Zip _____

BEGINNINGS

A Collection of Appetizers Presented by the

Junior League of Akron
929 West Market Street • Akron, Ohio 44313

(330) 836-4905

Please send _____ copies of *Beginnings* . . . . $22.95 each $ _____

Postage and handling. . . . . . $4.00 first book/$2.00 each additional book $ _____

Ohio residents add 5.75% sales tax (or current tax rate) $ _____

Total $ _____

Name _____

Address _____

City _____ State _____ Zip _____

Proceeds from the sale of this book support the Junior League of Akron, Ohio, Inc. and its good works.
Please allow 6 weeks for delivery.